Story Power!

Compelling Illustrations for Preaching and Teaching

James A. Feehan

Resource Publications, Inc.
San Jose, California

Editorial director: Kenneth Guentert
Managing editor: Elizabeth J. Asborno
Editorial assistants: Joyce Swanson, Susan Pellant

Originally published as *Stories for Preachers*, Dublin,
Ireland, Mercier Press, © 1988 James Feehan.

Reprint Department
Resource Publications, Inc.
160 E. Virginia Street #290,
San Jose, CA 95112-5876

Library of Congress Cataloging in Publication Data
Feehan, James A.
    [Stories for preachers]
    Story power! : compelling illustrations for preaching and
teaching / James Feehan.
        p.   cm.
    Originally published: Stories for preachers. Dublin :
Mercier Press ; U.S. distributor, Dufour Editions, c1989.
    Includes bibliographical references and index.
    ISBN 0-89390-304-3
    1. Preaching. 2. Storytelling—Religious aspects—
Christianity. 3. Homiletical illustrations. 4. Catholic
Church—Anecdotes. 5. Christian life—Anecdotes.
6. Feehan, James A. Stories for preachers. I. Title
BV4225.2.F44 1994
251'.08—dc 20   94-28674

Printed in the United States of America

98 97 96 95 94 | 5 4 3 2 1

To the memory of
Cardinal Peter McKeefry,
who had a story to tell
and a song to sing

I cannot hear a sermon without being struck by the fact that amid drowsy series of sentences what a sensation a historical fact, biographical name, a sharply objective illustration makes! Why will not the preacher heed the admonition of the momentary silence of his congregation (and often what is shown him) that this particular sentence is all they carry away?

Ralph Waldo Emerson (1803-1882)

Contents

Acknowledgments

The author and publisher would like to thank the following authors, publishers and copyrightholders for their permission to quote material for which they hold the copyright.

Richard Scott Simon Ltd. for material from *Night* by Elie Wiesel, Penguin Books, 1981.

Pantheon Books for material from Martin Buber's *Tales of the Hasidim* translated by Olga Marx, © Schocken Books, published by Pantheon Books a Division of Random House Inc.

Paulist Press for material reprinted from *Sir, We would like to see Jesus* by Walter J. Burghardt, S.J., © 1982 by the Author, and *Sunday After Sunday* by Robert Waznak, © 1983 by the Author. Used by permission of Paulist Press.

Veritas Publications for material from *Miracles Do Happen* by Briege McKenna.

Twenty-Third Publications for material reprinted with permission from *Storytelling: Imagination and Faith,* (paper, $7.95) © 1984 by William Bausch, and *Take Heart Father: A Hope-Filled Vision for Today's Priest,* © 1986 by William Bausch, (paper $9.95) published by Twenty-Third Publications, P.O. Box 180, Mystic, CT 06355. Distributed in Ireland and the UK by Columba Book Service, 93 The Rise, Mount Merrion, Blackrock, Co. Dublin.

Alba House for material from *Go Tell Everyone* by James McKarns.

Edward England Books for material from *The Craft of Sermon Illustration* by W. E. Sangster, published by Epworth Press, 1954. Reprinted with permission.

Tabor Publishing and Mark Link for material from *Illustrated Sunday Homilies* by Fr. Mark Link, © 1987 by Tabor Publishing, 25115 Avenue Stanford, Valencia, CA. 91355 United States. Used with permission.

Acknowledgments

A. D. Peters & Co. Ltd. for material from *An Only Child* by Frank O'Connor, published by Pan Books, reprinted by permission of A. D. Peters & Co. Ltd.

Marshall Pickering for material from *Issues Facing Christians Today* by John Stott, published by Marshall, Morgan & Scott, Basingstoke.

Gill and Macmillian for material from *In Monavalla* by Joseph Brady.

America for permission to quote one verse from *A Kind of Prayer* by Cyril Egan.

Hodder and Stoughton Ltd. for permission to quote material from Billy Graham's *Approaching Hoofbeats,* Hodder and Stoughton, London 1963.

The Bible Societies for quotations from the *Good News Bible,* published by the Bible Societies and Collins, © American Bible Society 1976.

Fr. William Burridge for his story of Shaka.

Collins Publishers for material from *The Case Against God* by Gerald Priestland, Collins, London 1984.

C.S.S. Publishing Company for permission to paraphrase and condense material from *Seldom Told Bible Tales: Fifteen Eye-opening Stories from the Old and New Testaments and the Apocrypha* by James McKarns, © 1985 C.S.S. Publishing Company. Used with permission of the publisher.

Every effort has been made to trace the owners of copyrighted material and it is hoped that no copyright has been infringed. If we have inadvertently infringed on any copyright we apologize and will make the necessary correction at the first opportunity.

Introduction

Beware of any course on "How to Preach: By One
Who Knows." The creature is an impostor! No man
knows how to preach. It is one thing to learn the
technique and mechanics of preaching: it is quite
another to preach a sermon which will draw back the
veil and make the barriers fall that hide the face of
God.   *James S. Stewart*

T'is only a mixem gatherem." This would have been an ideal
title for what follows were it not that it is already patented
by my housekeeper, Lena. She invariably uses it to introduce
the Monday luncheon menu which, more often than not,
consists of remnants of the cordon bleu Sunday offering with
a few of her own unique specialities thrown in for good
measure. "Sure 'twill do!" she says as she planks it down in
front of me and thereby hangs the first tale in this collection.
In our seminary days we had to submit a number of written
sermons to the professor of sacred eloquence. On one occasion a student was summoned to the august presence to
account for his effort. He felt uneasy about his text and his
fears were not allayed by the grim look on the professor's face
as he perused the manuscript. "'Twill do, Father?" he faltered.
"'Twill do, won't it?"

"Do what?" was the caustic reply.

The idea behind this book was first conceived by my
brother, Seán Feehan of the Mercier Press, who is quite a
seanchaí in his own right. For years we have been swapping
stories and once when we were discussing the new emphasis
on storytelling as part of our cultural and religious heritage he
suggested that I put together a collection of stories and

anecdotes which might be of some use in illustrating the Sunday homily. This "mixem gatherem" is the result, and now I wait in fear and trembling to see if "'twill do!" And as I wait I keep asking myself, "Do what?"

Let me stress at the outset that the views on preaching expressed here are impressionistic, and impressions are of necessity personal. It is not a book on storytelling as such. The theology and spirituality of story are a gigantic exercise for which I have neither the taste nor the competence. There are recognized experts in this field already. Fr. John Shea's *Stories of God* and *Stories of Faith* are classics of the storytelling process as also is William Bausch's *Storytelling—Imagination and Faith*.

We must constantly bear in mind that our faith started in storytelling. "In the past God spoke to our ancestors many times and in many ways through the prophets, but in these last days he has spoken to us through his Son" (Heb 1:1-2). And how did Jesus speak to us? He spoke in stories. He was the storyteller *par excellence*. His stories are from real life: stories about farming and fishing, weddings and funerals, saints and hypocrites, prodigal sons and self-righteous humbugs. He taught and he preached in pictures. "He would not speak to them without using parable" (Mk 4:34).

During the period of oral tradition his stories were told and retold and when the first gospel came to be written its most striking characteristic was its vivid storytelling. Mark was a born storyteller who filled his pages with unforgettable pictures. So the story came first and theology second. The latter really began as a reflection on story and in due course creeds, dogmas and catechisms were super-imposed on the storytelling process. There is now a notable revival in storytelling, a shift from the dogmas and creeds which dominated our thought patterns in the past, to what is now called narrative theology.

Thank God I have experienced this transition in a ministry which has passed largely from a word culture into an image culture where the Christian message must be presented visually if it is to gain access to the minds and hearts in the pews.

Introduction

Billions are spent every year on the visual, whether it be television, theater, concerts or films. Young people study to stereo and they will skip Mass when U2 comes to Dublin or Cork. It is reckoned that the child will spend ten years of its life in front of the television. Even the commercials bombard us with a flood of imaginative talent in the sale of their products.

That is part of the challenge facing us in getting the message across on Sundays. We have, to no little extent, hidden Christ in the jargon. People will no longer buy unctuous phrases like "dearly beloved brethren" and "Holy Mother Church" or have chunks of dogma thrown at them in archaic and therefore unintelligible terminology. "I have sat," writes a contributor to *Worship and Preaching*, "through services where rows of bored young faces testify that the preacher's thoughts were divorced from the thoughts of inquiring adolescents."

The Second Vatican Council tells us that the homily should proclaim, represent and make effectively present "God's wonderful works in the history of salvation." To find these wonderful works we draw on the Scriptures. Nowadays, however, it cannot be assumed that the sermon emerges from Scripture as a flower emerges from a bud. Ireland's most popular television program, *The Late Late Show,* recently celebrated twenty-five years of unbroken production. Amongst the many tributes to the compère and producer was one from a cleric who claimed that the show had given half the priests of the country subject-matter for their Sunday sermons. He was referring to some of the controversial issues regularly aired on the program. Too often the basis of a sermon is a television program, a newspaper article, or an event of local or world importance. When this happens the sheep are not fed. What should have been an illustration—the television program or newspaper article—becomes the theme and the Scripture —which should have been the theme—becomes an illustration that is lucky to get in at all.

It should never be forgotten that the message is what matters most, and the only value that sermon illustrations can have is to light up the message. The story must always be subservient to the message. It should make the message come alive and above all evoke a religious response. I am under no illusions about the shortcomings of this collection. Illustrations have a way of becoming "dated," the more attractive ones tend to become hackneyed, and in churches where the preachers change frequently we can never be sure that the same illustration has not been used the week before.

One one occasion the priest conducting a diocesan retreat told a nice little story that had a good punchline in it. One of his listeners used it with great effect in a parish where he visited one Sunday. The trouble was, however, that this particular parish had a succession of priests visiting each Sunday and when three or four others had tried the same story it began to lose some of its luster, much to the amusement of the congregation. Eventually when one particular man used it there were smiles all over the church. After Mass one of the congregation came into the sacristy and congratulated him on his "grand sermon" adding: "I'll put it to you this way, Father. Of all the eight men who told that story over the past six months, you told it the best."

What about humor? Ours is a religion of joy, so an occasional ripple of laughter can provide welcome relaxation, assuming of course that the illustration is relevant to the message. To tell a funny story because it is a funny story is to trivialize preaching. The aim should be to feed the sheep, not amuse the goats! "Take a leaf out of Shakespeare's book," writes Donald Coggan in *The Sacrament of the Word.* "He knew the wisdom of bringing the fool on the stage from time to time: the audience needed relief from the pressure of high drama; laughter would provide it. A touch of humor providing it is relevant to the subject in hand gives a rest, a breathing space to the congregation."

Preachers today are more and more making the story or "picture" the heart of their approach to homiletic preparation. I would hope that some of the stories and anecdotes in this book may be of help to those who like myself have the awesome privilege of publicly proclaiming Christ's message and perhaps sow the seeds from which their own creative thoughts will develop.

By way of an apologia for what follows, let me quote Jack Point, the Jester in *Yeomen of the Guard*:

> O winnow all my folly and you'll find...
> A grain or two of truth among the chaff.

If the reader should come across a grain or two of truth in what follows, then no more need be said to justify this "mixem gatherem."

1. The Legacy of Nathan

A story is the shortest distance between a human
being and truth.   *Anthony De Mello*

O ne of the great stories in our religious tradition is the one
told three thousand years ago by the Jewish prophet
Nathan. He told it in order to catch the conscience of King
David.

There was a sex scandal in high places. It involved the king,
who had an affair with a married woman. When she informed
him that she was pregnant he arranged to have her husband
killed. After the murder, for such it was, he took the woman,
Bathsheba, as his wife. David was guilty of two crimes, murder
and adultery, the second carrying a mandatory death sentence
which he somehow escaped. But he did not escape the wrath
of God. It came in a dramatic confrontation with the Lord's
spokesman, Nathan. Nathan's technique as he confronted
David with his sin was masterly in its dramatic effect. He told
David the following story:

"There were two men who lived in the same town; one was
rich and the other poor. The rich man had many cattle and
sheep, while the poor man had only one lamb, which he had
bought. He took care of it, and it grew up in his home with
his children. He would feed it with some of his own food, let
it drink from his cup, and hold it in his lap. The lamb was like
a daughter to him. One day a visitor arrived at the rich man's
home. The rich man didn't want to kill one of his own animals
to prepare a meal for him; instead, he took the poor man's
lamb and cooked a meal for his guest."

David was very angry with the rich man and said, "I swear
by the living Lord that the man who did this ought to die! For

1

having done such a cruel thing, he must pay back four times as much as he took."

"You are that man," Nathan said to David (2 Sam 12:1-7).

David's response to the story was one simple sentence, "I have sinned against the Lord."

This sentence forms the core of Psalm 51, the great "Miserere" psalm in which David confronts himself with his own sinfulness and his need of God's saving mercy. In this wonderful hymn of repentance, David is restored to fellowship with God, and for that reason he is still looked upon as the greatest king ever to reign over Israel.

Nathan inherited and bequeathed a rich legacy of stories. He belonged to a people who were the first to acknowledge the one true God. The Jews were the people who gave the world Abraham, Moses, Jesus, Mary, and the Twelve Apostles. They gave us two-thirds of the bible, which is in itself an anthology of stories. It is not surprising, then, that for our illustrations we should be tapping our Jewish heritage, and let's not forget that it is our heritage. Jewish tradition has kept up its storytelling propensities right down through the ages. Robin Flower often recalled a story he heard from a *seanchaí* on the Blasket Islands. He identified it instantly as one told by the Jew Petrus in Arabia in the eleventh century: "It had found its way to this westernmost of all European land," he said, adding, "and was probably assisted in its migration by the fact that is was a rather improper tale!"

Their story tradition was undimmed even in the darkest periods of history.

Here is a delightful story from the rabbinic collection which can be used to great effect to illustrate married love. Joachim and Rebecca were married for about ten years but there was no sign of a child to gladden Joachim's heart and perpetuate his name. So he decided to divorce his wife and went to old Rabbi Ben Shamir to make the necessary arrangements. "Joachim son," said the Rabbi, "we had a party to celebrate your marriage, so before we do anything about the divorce we're going to have another party to mark your parting," and unknown to Joachim, he winked knowingly at Rebecca.

The party came, and acting on the advice of the Rabbi, Rebecca plied her beloved with the best vintage wine. As she topped off the cup Joachim spoke to her, "Little wife, take what you like best from this place and take it with you to your father's house." Then he fell asleep. Rebecca put him to bed and then with the connivance of the Rabbi and the sturdy shoulders of some of the guests they brought the bed with Joachim in it to her father's house.

When he woke the following morning and recognized the surroundings he called Rebecca. "Little wife, what am I doing here?" to which she coyly replied: "I only did what you told me to, husband dear. I took what I liked best to my father's house—and that was you!" Joachim took her in his arms and forgot about the divorce.

A few weeks later she told him she was pregnant.

There is a story of a rabbi and a cantor and a humble synagogue cleaner who were preparing for the Day of Atonement. The rabbi beat his breast, and said, "I am nothing, I am nothing." The cantor beat his breast and said ,"I am nothing, I am nothing." The cleaner beat his breast, and said, "I am nothing, I am nothing." And the rabbi said to the cantor, "Look who thinks he's nothing!"

1. The Legacy of Nathan

The richness of Nathan's legacy is powerfully illustrated in this story by Martin Buber:

"My grandfather was lame. Once he was asked to tell a story about his teacher, and he told how the Holy Bal Shem Tove used to jump and dance when he was praying. My grandfather stood up while he was telling the story and the story carried him away so much that he had to jump and dance to show how the master did it. From that moment he was healed." This is how stories ought to be told.

The grandfather was healed by the power of the story because he recognized the story as his own. That is the challenge facing the preacher—to tell the story of God in such a way that the listener will identify his or her own story with it. The storyteller has to bring the *then* of Nathan's to the *now* of our own story.

On Good Friday the priests and parishioners of Thurles departed from the traditional manner of doing the Way of the Cross in the churches and took the stations on to the streets of the town. The *then* of God's story in Jerusalem became the *now* on the Via Dolorosa of a Tipperary town. The storyteller has to listen to the people's stories and think of the *then* in terms of the *now* if he or she is be an effective narrator of God's story. That is Nathan's legacy.

But that is not all we owe to our Jewish heritage. If there is one dominant characteristic of the times in which we live it must surely be a sense of hopelessness. Like the disciples on the Emmaus Road, we seem to have turned our backs on Jerusalem and lost hope. The crime wave has hit our world with hurricane force, one third of the world goes to bed hungry, and there is the threat of nuclear catastrophe. But throughout the dark vicissitudes of their history the Jewish people preserved undimmed the torch of hope. For them it was always "next year in Jerusalem." Recently the Russian dissident Scharansky was reunited with his wife in Jerusalem. It was a happy ending to a story of hope. The following report of his speech from the dock was reported world-wide by the media at the time of his trial some years ago.

"I am happy. I am happy that I lived honestly in and with my conscience. I never compromised my soul, even under the threat of death.

"For more than 2,000 years the Jewish people, my people, have lived in dispersal. But wherever they are, wherever Jews are found, every year they repeat: 'Next Year, In Jerusalem.'

"Now when I am further than ever from my people, from my Avital (his wife's nickname), facing many arduous years of imprisonment, I say, turning to my people, to my Avital: 'Next year, in Jerusalem.'

"Now I turn to the court which is required to confirm a predetermined judgment. To you, I have nothing to say."

The dissidents—Jews, Christians and atheists—wept and applauded and sang the "Hatikvah," the Israeli anthem whose name, translated, means "hope."

Ireland too has a rich legacy of stories and storytellers. The *seanchaí* "storyteller" is part of our cultural heritage. The storyteller's speech is illustrated with stories long, short and tall which come naturally with the flow of conversation and stem from a vast flood of tradition which was still a living force when Irish was the spoken language, but which has now to a great extent vanished like the snows of yesteryear.

Between 1910 and 1930 Robin Flower made many visits to the Great Blasket Island which lies three miles out into the Atlantic off the coast of County Kerry and there by the turf fires of a small fishing community he discovered a vast lore of stories, some of which he has preserved for posterity. Many of these stories owe their origins to what Flower describes as the "university of the road."

> The tales spread among the people of the roads, the wandering harvesters, the tramping men and the beggars, the poor scholars and poets and migratory schoolmasters...and if we find, as I have found on the Island, a tale which can be traced back, through the jest books of the Middle Ages and the sermon books of the preaching friars to the Arabs of Africa, and through Persian books to ancient India, it is by such men that it has been carried from extremest east to farthest west, to die at last by a turf fire within hearing of the Atlantic wave.

Flower's beloved islanders no longer live on the Great Blasket. Their sons and daughters have turned to a new way of life on the mainland but their heritage lives on in the writings of their greatest storytellers—Tomás Ó Criomhthain and Peig Sayers. As for the others, Ireland is the poorer for their passing.

2. Bored to Death

Paul spoke to the people and kept on speaking until
midnight.   *Acts 20:7*

Eutychus loved a good story. After all, he grew up in Troas,
which was once the proud city of Troy. Time and again
he heard the gripping story of how Paris, Prince of Troy, stole
Helen, the world's most beautiful woman, from her husband
and brought her to this historic city, thus setting off the fierce
and bloody Trojan war. He would have heard the tale of the
Trojan horse with the Greek soldiers hiding inside, which
eventually led to the capture and destruction of Troy. And in
more recent times he would have seen for himself the House
of the Apparition, where the Macedonian appeared to the
traveling preacher Paul, inviting him to introduce the Christian
faith to Europe.

This was a special Sunday for Eutychus because Paul was
in town for what was to be his last visit to Troas. The word
was out that he would be preaching at the Evening Eucharist
and Eutychus was determined to get a good look at the great
man. A large crowd had already gathered at the church when
he arrived, so priding himself on his ability as a climber he got
himself on to the sill of an open window three stories up and
there he sat, legs dangling, awaiting the arrival of the famous
apostle.

Then Paul arrived to a tumultuous welcome from the people
of the Christian community he had founded. When the ap-
plause died down he began to preach, but before long it was
perfectly clear that not even Paul was going to hold the
sustained attention of the hyperactive young man on the
window sill. As Paul went on and on, Eutychus got more and

more bored. The oil lamps were lit, emitting an odor, and the sermon still went on. Poor Eutychus began to nod; next thing he dozed off and there was a loud commotion as he fell to the ground three floors below. There was a doctor in the house at the time, Luke, Paul's friend and fellow-traveler. Paul, unaware that he had bored one of his congregation to death, was summoned to the scene and he restored the young man to life.

This seldom-told bible story (Acts 20) will give some comfort to those of us who hear the occasional snore from the pews. After all, if Paul couldn't keep them interested, what hope for me!

It is significant that Luke who was an eye-witness does not record one word of Paul's marathon sermon. He just says, Paul went on and on!

In these days of centrally heated churches, foam-rubber kneeling pads and TV-saturated congregations with tabloid newspapers awaiting them at the church gates, one is inclined to go along with whoever expressed the view that if it can't be said in five minutes it can't be said in fifty-five! We must face the reality of the situation as it is today. The short sermon may well call for more preparation than the one which meanders on. The Duke of Wellington apologized for the length of his dispatches saying, "I had not time to make them shorter."

The interest span of modern audiences is not nearly as extended as it once was. Television hits us with commercials just about every ten to twelve minutes and people in general can manage little more than that in sustained concentration. The story is told of one preacher who, like St. Paul, went on and on for the best part of half an hour. Leaving the church after Mass he came upon two ladies at the holy water font so deeply engrossed in conversation they were oblivious of his presence. As one of them blessed herself she confided to the other, "Another sermon like that, Molly alanna, and sure we won't feel the winter!"

This makes it absolutely imperative that we put careful thought and preparation into what we have to say. "Four hours preparation, for every minute in the pulpit," so writes Walter Burghardt, SJ, who goes on to explain that this includes reading, prayer, reflection, writing and re-writing. Writing is important. This does not mean that we write, slavishly memorize, and then repeat by rote what we've written. We are preachers, not announcers! It does ensure, however, that we have one central message with a beginning, middle, and end.

Ronald Knox was a brilliant preacher who always brought the text of his sermon into the pulpit with him and used it in such a way that it never became a distraction nor created a barrier in communication. On one occasion he was chided by a bishop for taking his manuscript into the pulpit. The prelate labored the point a bit too long and provoked the following retort from Knox: "Ah yes, my Lord, I recognize the validity of your observations. I sensed it one day when I was about to mount the pulpit with my manuscript in my hand and I heard a gentleman in the first pew whisper to his wife, 'My God, another bloody pastoral'!"

The challenge to the preacher is an awesome one. Gone are the days when he was one of the few people in the community with above-average education. He now faces people many of whom possess higher academic qualifications than he does; people with discerning, inquiring minds, who come in the expectation of getting something from the liturgy; people with different wants, different needs. They may be attending from habit, but habit or no habit, they bring with them their anxieties, illnesses, worries, hurts and hopes for a healing word, a thought from a homily, something that will lift them up, carry them on and give them the strength to bear the unhappiness they suffer at the present time. This is the challenge: to find the words and speak them in such a way that the message will have some relevance for the range of souls before us.

Remember Milton's scathing indictment of the preacher of his day:

> The hungry sheep look up and are not fed,
> But swollen with wind and the rank mist they
>   draw,
> Rot inwardly, and foul contagion spread.

Ultimately what counts is the effort we put into preparing and proclaiming the Word and the love that motivates our work.

There's another story about a famous preacher. The trouble was that he knew he was an excellent speaker and he used his sermons to build his reputation. At the end of his life as he lay dying it was clear that something was deeply troubling him. A priest friend who sat by his bedside saw this and said, "Take heart, Father John. When you go before the Lord to be judged, just remind him of all those wonderful sermons you preached."

Father John replied, "If the Lord doesn't mention them, I certainly won't remind him of them."

3. Breaking Bread in Galilee

To be ignorant of the Scriptures is to be ignorant of
Christ.   *St. Jerome*

The Lake of Galilee in Christ's own country must be one of
the most beautiful spots on this earth. The first time I saw
it was at Capernaum. It was evening and the sun was setting
behind the hills of Tiberias, throwing a golden hue across the
lake. As we boarded a boat to cross to the other side, an old
priest on his way back to India threw out his arms and
exclaimed, "The Good Lord knew what he was at when he
chose this place!"

On the last evening of our visit I was sitting on the terrace
of our hotel in Tiberias, looking out at the lake. It was night
and this time it was the moon that cast a golden track across
the waters. There was a sense of Christ about the place. It was
one of the few scenes that had not suffered the ravages of
time. A voice behind me said, "It is good for us to be here!"
Turning, I saw a white-haired gentleman with a kindly face. I
recognized him as one of our group. He was a shopkeeper
from Cork and a Protestant to boot. He handed me a sheet of
paper. "Father, you might like to take a look at that. It's a bit
of a poem I put together about all the wonderful places we've
seen." So it was. Each verse recalled memories of a holy place
and the last line was the same. Here's what he wrote on
Galilee—a simple little poem with no pretensions to great art:

O, Lord, when I think of Galilee,
I think of disciples afloat.
I think of loaves and fishes
I think of Peter's boat.

I think of you walking on water
I think of a stormy sea
But Lord when I think of Galilee
I think most of all of Thee!

There were about nine verses in all and I noticed that each line had a cross reference to the Scripture text on which it was based.

"How long have you been reading the Scriptures?" I asked.

"Ever since I was a teenager," he replied. "I was browsing through the bible one day and an unfamiliar name caught my eye. Then I suddenly said to myself: supposing I get to heaven and a little man comes up to me and introduces himself to me as Obadiah, and seeing me nonplussed adds: 'I wrote one of the books of the bible,' I'd have to confess that not alone had I not read his book but I'd never heard of the man himself. That set me off. Now I have about three thousand books on the Scriptures."

When I asked him how he'd break the bread of God's word with a beginner he said, "We're all beginners. We all have to put up L-Plates where this book is concerned."

Then he proceeded to give me three L-Plates. "This book," he said, "is first of all *love-giving*—every page is about God's love for us; then it is *life-giving*—'These have been written in order that you may believe that Jesus is the Messiah, the Son of God, and that through your faith in him you may have life!' (Jn 20:31); and finally it is *liberty-giving*—'you will know the truth, and the truth will set you free' (Jn 8:32). We're all slaves you know," he added, "to pleasure, power, possessions. This is a word from the beyond telling us how to cast off the chains. Whenever I open this book," he concluded, "it is to find Jesus. The *Old Testament* was written because he was coming, the *New Testament* because he came. It's as simple as that!"

I once used this incident as an opening to a sermon on the Scriptures. A young girl came to me afterward and told me that it was the first time she'd ever heard a sermon about the bible in a Catholic church. She had been toying with the idea of joining a cult called The Way International. Some members of this group had introduced her to the Scriptures, which up to then had just been a school subject, an exam to be passed. No one had ever explained to her that the God-ordained purpose of Scripture is to point and lead people to Christ.

I could readily emphasize with her because that memorable breaking of the bread of God's word with a Cork business man by the Sea of Galilee had radically changed my approach to the Scriptures. In the seminary I saw it as simply another course to be done, a useful source for scoring points in dogma. As a priest I wouldn't touch a commentary for preaching purposes, my main source of information being the many pre-packaged "homily hints." Christ's constant complaint to the religious leaders of his day, "Have you not read...?" fell on deaf ears. It all fell into place, however, in the most pungent of those complaints: "You study the Scriptures because you think that in them you will find eternal life. And these very Scriptures speak about me! Yet you are not willing to come to me in order to have life" (Jn 5:39).

The Second Vatican Council has left us with no choice but to be steeped in the Scriptures if we are to be effective preachers. It tells us to read Scripture diligently and study it carefully lest any of us become "an empty preacher of the word of God outwardly who is not a listener to it inwardly." The Council further insists that "all the preaching of the Church must be nourished and ruled by Sacred Scripture" (*Divine Revelation*, Article 21).

We must face the fact that the expository preaching of the Scriptures is hampered by the virtual non-existence of biblical knowledge in the great majority of people who listen to us on Sundays. Ignorance of Scripture is something that has to be tackled sometime, somewhere, somehow. Bible study groups may be part of the solution. In the meantime, however, the preacher who attempts to expound the written Word can assume nothing. Agatha Christie tells the story of a young cleric who in the course of a sermon pointed a finger at a handful of simple people in the front pews. "Ha!" he said accusingly, "I know what you're thinking. You think that the Xerxes mentioned in the Second Book of the Kings was Artaxerxes the first. Well, you're wrong! He was Artaxerxes the second!"

And, talking about the Old Testament, people are often turned off by the language, imagery and thought forms of the first reading, which are sometimes light years away from those with which they have to do in the world of today. How to build a bridge between these entirely different worlds is a challenge facing the preacher. Because the circumstances in which the prophets found themselves were vastly different from those confronting us in the late twentieth century, the preacher has to try to discover what was there in their teaching that was timeless, deliver it in simple and vivid language, and apply it to the contemporary situation.

Accommodating the Scriptures to bolster the preacher's preconceived ideas or personal hang-ups is a pit-fall to be avoided at all cost. According to Raymond Brown, "Occasional use of the imagination in accommodating Scripture can be attractive, but to substitute it for the literal sense is to substitute the man's ingenuity for God's inspired Word."

Once I was on a night-flight home from Lourdes. Behind me was an old man who had never been on a plane before this, his first visit to Lourdes. As the aircraft taxied down the runway for take-off he looked out into the night and exclaimed, "Well, how will he make his way home in the dark?" It was explained to him that all he had to do was place his trust in the captain. He would guide him safely home.

The bible is like that. It can guide us to a home we cannot see. If we follow it, it will reveal to us Christ, the Way, who will take us safely home to the Father.

4. The Door

The word of God, as far as I am concerned, is
something which is absolutely precious. It means an
awful lot to me. You have asked me to come along
tomorrow to go out and read something I have never
seen before. If I were doing a television program I
would spend a whole week preparing it. I will not go
out there just to read in front of people without
putting a lot of preparation into it, without having it
explained to me. I want to know what it is about. I
want to know what the people are to get out of it. I
want to pray about it.   *Eamon Andrews*

A famous English preacher was invited to speak at the
dedication of a new cathedral in the United States. As he
gazed around the modern edifice he muttered to the one sitting
beside him, "I cannot preach here. The walls do not speak to
me."

The liturgical symbols of the church building can often
provide the preacher with useful visual stimuli in illustrating
his message. Cathedrals like Chartres and Milan are veritable
sermons in stone. Thurles Cathedral has a wealth of liturgical
symbols which I have found effective in illustrating the Sunday
homily. The most attractive and artistic feature of the cathedral
is the seemingly infinite variety of precious marbles. Oldest
amongst them is a green slab of Africano marble set in the
floor in front of the tabernacle. It was quarried by Christian
slaves in the second century and was the gift of Pope Puis IX.
Supporting the main edifice are giant marble columns of
Kilkenny black, Cork red, Galway green and Sicilian white.
Black is a type of sin; red pictures the blood of Jesus; the white
marble indicates cleansing by that precious blood; and the

4. The Door

green symbolizes new life springing from the outpouring of the Spirit at Pentecost.

On a visit to Cologne, Mark Link found a telling illustration of the Bread of Life on the door of a church. The door had four panels, each portraying a biblical scene relating to the Eucharist. The first panel had six stone jars, depicting the miracle at Cana where Jesus changed water into wine; the second showed five loaves and two fishes, referring to the feeding of the five thousand; the third panel portrayed Jesus and the Twelve seated at a table in the Upper Room; and the last panel had three figures—Jesus breaking bread with the two disciples in the inn at Emmaus. Then on four successive Sundays the priest, taking each panel in turn, explained to his people the message on the door.

The first panel shows the changing of water into wine at Cana. The common interpretation of this miracle is that the Lord came to the rescue of a young couple who found themselves in the embarrassing situation of having run out of liquid refreshments for their guests. The artist's message was that just as Jesus had turned water into wine so one day he would change wine into his blood, thus prefiguring the Eucharist.

The second panel shows the promise of the Eucharist in the feeding of the five thousand. In Capernaum he gave ordinary bread; at the Last Supper he would give the Bread of Life. In the multiplication of the loaves he provided for physical hunger; in the Eucharist he would satisfy the hunger of the spirit.

The third panel reveals the institution of the Eucharist. In the Upper Room Jesus does more than change water into wine; he changes wine into his blood. He does more than multiply the loaves; he changes bread into his body. This panel tells the people what the Mass is all about.

We move to the final panel and in the meal at Emmaus we see the first post-resurrection Eucharist. Luke uses the language of the Last Supper when he tells us how Jesus "took the bread and said the blessing, then he broke the bread and gave it to them" (Lk 24:30).

4. The Door

In this Emmaus incident Jesus revealed himself to the disciples in two ways. First, in the Scriptures. He explained to them everything the Scriptures had to say about himself and afterward they recalled how their hearts were burning as he explained the Scriptures to them. Then in the inn their eyes were opened and they recognized him in the breaking of the bread. We have been taught that Christ reveals himself to us in every Mass in the liturgy of the Eucharist. Isn't it strange that so few of us ever find him, particularly in the word as it is proclaimed and preached on Sundays. Indigestible chunks from the Old Testament tend to switch us off at the outset. The responsorial psalm, the purpose of which is to make the word of God real flesh in our lives, evokes such a feeble response. "For you my soul is thirsting, O Lord, my God"—am I really thirsting? Can I sign my name at the bottom of the psalm? The gospel is frequently followed by an unrelated homily with a spate of announcements thrown in for good measure. Do we honestly expect the people to find Christ in all of this? The answer to the problem may be found in those chilling words of Christ addressed to the Jews: "He who comes from God listens to God's words. You, however, are not from God, and that is why you will not listen" (Jn 8:47).

What he is telling them is that they have shut their hearts against God's indwelling Spirit. We cannot experience the Lord's presence in his Word unless there is something within us to respond to it. The blockages, barriers and resistances are so often within ourselves. Part of the explanation may rest in the manner in which the Word is proclaimed. The following illustration is based on a recent experience.

One evening a couple came to me to talk over their marriage ceremony and in the course of the discussion I asked if they had given any thought to the readings. Getting a negative response I gave them a booklet containing the lectionary selection and suggested some passages which might appeal to them. When I asked, "What about a reader?" the bride replied chirpily, "Pa Joe might do it because he was stuck with it the last time." Sensing my uneasiness, she went on to reassure me that there would be no need to go over the readings with Pa Joe because "he got through it fine last time." Nevertheless I still had a grim sense of foreboding on the big day as I invited the guests to sit and listen to the Word of God. I then gave the nod to Pa Joe, who emerged from his seat and approached the ambo, rooting in his pockets for what I thought might be his glasses but what turned out to be a crumpled piece of paper from which he proceeded to "do" the readings. I write these lines just five hours after the ceremony and I can truthfully say that all I can recall from Pa Joe's proclaiming of the Word of the Lord is the sense of relief with which he gave his valedictory: This is the Word of the Lord. Skipping the Alleluia verse he stepped down from the ambo, crumpling his script as he returned to his seat.

If there is one area in our ministry where we must thump our breasts in repentance it must surely be in the selection and preparation of lay readers. How often do we tear around the parish on Saturday armed with missalettes looking for someone to "do" the readings the following day or telling them they're "on" for the coming month. The text at the beginning of this chapter is part of a reply given by Eamon Andrews to a priest who sent an altar boy to his home on Saturday to tell him he was "on" at the eleven o'clock Mass next morning. Sometimes when the regular reader fails to turn up, an unsuspecting worshiper has a missalette thrust on him or her with the words, "Will you do it?" I've seen a reader who was presumably at an earlier Mass disappearing through the sacristy during the gospel, having done his duty!

By way of postscript let me mention another role of the laity which has its problems. There are still some, in decreasing numbers, thank God, who will not accept communion from a lay minister. The following letter addressed to one such appeared recently in a parish newsletter:

"I wonder what you were thinking when you crossed over from my line to Father's! That I was unworthy to hand you the Bread of Life? Of course I'm unworthy! So also, for that matter, is Father. Were you thinking of my hands, that they were not fit to touch the Body of Christ? These hands have changed more than thirty thousand diapers, they have brought comfort and healing to others at home and in hospital and in so doing have touched the Body of Christ. I know they are unworthy to touch the Lord's Body, but then...whose are?"

5. The Search for God

I sought my soul, but my soul I could not see,
I sought my God, but my God eluded me,
I sought my brother, and I found all three.

Anonymous

"A Kind of Prayer" is a poem by Cyril Egan on the search for God. It is about a man who is forever looking for something. One day someone asks him what he is looking for. "I'm looking for God," he replies, adding quickly:

Don't tell me I'll find him in my heart,
(though in a sense that's true;)
And don't tell me I'll find him in my fellow man,
(Though in a sense that's true too;)
What I'm looking for is a God
Making a five-sense breakthrough to humanity.

He is looking for a God whom he can touch and see and feel—in other words, an experience of God. How seldom, if ever, do we preach on the problem of unbelief, and yet people are constantly coming to us with serious doubts about the existence of God! We must surely have some message for them. I know of one instance where a woman troubled with problems of faith came to a priest and asked him desperately if there was anything she could do. His reply surprised her. "There is," he said. "How about trying to love your neighbor a little bit better, in deeds rather than words? Put your heart into it." His advice ties in with John's words, "Whoever loves… knows God" (1 Jn 4:7).

5. The Search for God

In one of his plays Pádraig Pearse tells the story of Mac Dara, the Singer who returns home and tells his old school-teacher Maoilsheachlainn about his loss of faith. "Once, as I knelt by the cross of Kilgobbin, it became clear to me with an awful clearness, that there was no God. Why pray after that? I burst into a fit of laughter at the folly of men in thinking that there is a God. I felt inclined to run through the villages and cry aloud, 'People, it is all a mistake. There is no God...' Then I said, 'Why take away their illusion? If they find out that there is no God, their hearts will be as lonely as mine' so I walked the roads with my secret." To which Maoilsheachlainn replied, "Mac Dara, I am sorry for this. You must pray, you must pray. You will find God again. He has only hidden his face from you."

"No," said Mac Dara, "He has revealed His face to me...the people, Maoilsheachlainn, the dumb suffering people...In them I saw or seemed to see again the face of God."

In the people and his concern that his unbelief might disturb their simple faith, Mac Dara rediscovered the face of God.

There are some wonderful rabbinical stories about unbelief. One of them came from a German concentration camp in the Second World War. Amongst the inmates were a group of rabbis and learned Jews. They had to work for six-and-a-half days a week but on Sundays they were left in relative peace. One such afternoon some of the learned Jews in their despair decided to put God on trial. The rabbis acted as judges and witnesses came forward for the defense and for the prosecution.

The case for the prosecution was overwhelming. They had only to look around them: they were being wiped out as a race; many of their families had already died in the gas chambers. How could a good God allow this to happen?

21

The judges, despite a stout defense, had no difficulty in reaching a verdict. God was guilty as charged, guilty of abandoning his chosen people. Silence fell upon the court and then one elderly Jew got to his feet. "Nevertheless," he said, "let us not forget…It is time for our evening prayers!"

One of the rabbis who went through the hell of Auschwitz was Hugo Gryn. He tells of a rabbi in his synagogue in a small village in Poland. He was trying to conduct a service on the Sabbath but one of his congregation, the local tailor, was creating a disturbance, shaking his fist and muttering to himself and disturbing everyone around him. When the service was over the rabbi approached him and asked him what on earth was the matter.

"Ah!" says the tailor. "I got into a terrible argument with God. I said to him, 'Look, I know I am not perfect. There have been times when I sat down and had my meal without saying the blessing or the grace. And there have been days when I have hurried through my prayers. And I must confess that I have sometimes charged people for double thread when I only used single, and sometimes I have kept a bit of cloth back to make clothes for my own children. So I'm not claiming any special privileges. But you, God! You take babies away from their mothers. Young men die on the field of battle. People are cut down before their time through illness. How can you let this happen? So, let me make a bargain with you! If you'll forgive me, I'll forgive you."

And the tailor said to the rabbi, "Did I do wrong?"

"My friend, you had such a strong case, why did you let God off so easily?" the rabbi replied.

Atheism and agnosticism can often be chalked up to plain downright ignorance or laziness in thinking things out.

Once a young boy living in a village in Eastern Europe wanted to become an atheist but didn't know how to go about it. Someone told him about Jacob the Atheist who lived in another village about two hundred miles away and so the boy walked for days until he came to Jacob's village. When he found the house he was greeted by Jacob's wife who told him that Jacob was in the synagogue and wouldn't be back for a while.

Eventually Jacob came home and the boy said to him, "How come you've been to the synagogue and you're an atheist?"

"Yes of course I am," Jacob replied. "You see they need ten people for a quorum and they needed me, so of course I went. And then I went to a circumcision. It was my great honor to hold the baby for my friend, so of course I did it."

The boy then said, "But I want to be an atheist. How do I go about it?"

So Jacob said to him, "Tell me now, do you know the bible?"

"No, I want to be an atheist."

"Do you know the Talmud—the Law?" Jacob asked.

"Of course not. I have no time for that stuff," the boy replied.

So Jacob said finally, "Now listen, my dear boy. What you are is an ignoramus. To be an atheist you really have to have some knowledge."

This same Jacob caused quite a stir in his native village when it became known that he was an atheist. When the rabbi confronted him with the report at synagogue on the Sabbath, Jacob allayed his fears by saying, "Rabbi, do not believer every rumor you hear." The following day Jacob visited the rabbi and told him that he had decided to become an atheist. When asked why then he hadn't admitted it on the previous day, Jacob protested, "But rabbi, how could I tell you on the Sabbath!"

Here is a delightful story of an incident which could only happen in Italy. A woman was being harassed by a communist who was trying to prove to her that God did not exist. Eventually when he succeeded the woman wrung her arms and said, "All right, so there is no God! But there is always the Mother of God!"

The problem of unbelief often has its roots in the false images we have of God. There is God the stern ruler of the universe, way up there, remote and inaccessible, a God so remote that we cannot have a personal relationship with him. Then there is the image which is a carry-over from our childhood days—the Vindictive God, the eternal policeman ever vigilant, watching to catch us in the act. Once a little boy was caught with his hand in the cookie jar. His mother castigated him, "God is very angry with you. You'll pay for this...You just wait and see!" He was thereupon banished to his room to await the wrath of God. Shortly afterward there was a sudden thunderstorm and the mother ran to the boy's room to see if he was frightened. She found him looking out the window, munching one of the pilfered cookies and muttering to himself, "All this fuss over a few cookies!"

Once, mother went so far as to post a sign on the kitchen wall: GOD SEES YOU. Then Granny came on a visit and allayed the fears of the children. "Every time you read these words," she said, "try to remember that God loves you so much that he cannot take his eyes off you."

Tennyson once said that "the general English view of God is as an immeasurable clergyman," and Michael Paul Gallagher commenting on this says, "This God of the Institution seems to epitomize the foibles and failings of His official representatives: bossy, cranky, moody, peevish, fussy, petty, stuffy, petulant...all multiplied by infinity."

Once a little girl was absorbed with paper and pencil, drawing something. "What are you drawing today?" her mother asked her.

"God," was the reply.

"But you can't draw God, darling. No one knows what God is like."

"They will soon," said the little girl, "when I've done my drawing."

All down through the ages people have been "drawing God" in some form or another. Centuries ago in Athens they put up a statue "To the Unknown God."

Turgenev, the Russian novelist, tells how once when he was worshiping with peasants in a simple village church a man came up and stood by him. He had a face like all men's faces.

"Can this be Christ?" he said. "Such an ordinary, ordinary man. It cannot be!" Then at last the truth came home to him. "Only then I realized," he said, "that just such a face like all men's faces is the face of Christ."

A war story provided William Sangster with the picture he wanted in order to show that we see ourselves only when we see ourselves in Christ.

"During the war a soldier picked up on the battlefields of France a battered frame which had once contained a picture of Jesus. The picture had gone but the frame still bore the words: *Ecce Homo*. The soldier sent it home as a souvenir, and someone at home put a mirror in it and hung it on the wall. One day a man went into the house and understood the startling words 'Behold the man' and saw himself. We see ourselves only when we see ourselves in Jesus. Blots we barely knew there come to view in his white light."

When Yuri Gagarin, the Russian cosmonaut, returned to earth after man's first flight in space, he announced that he had not seen God "up there." The question "Where is God?" has yielded many answers and many stories.

There's a story about a tyrannical ruler who held his people in bondage but could not destroy their faith. One day he called his counselors together and asked their advice on where they might hide God so that the people would not find him.

One suggested that they hide him behind the stars, where he could not be reached. "No," said the ruler, "someday they'll conquer space and find him there."

Another suggested the bottom of the sea. "No," said the ruler again, "one day science and technology will plumb the depths of the ocean and he'll be found."

And then one wise old sage put forward his view. "Let's hide him among the people themselves," he advised, "that's the last place they'll ever think of looking for him."

Emmanuel, "God with us," is well illustrated by the following humorous story. An American was being shown around the Vatican and as the pope was out of town he was taken into the inner sanctum. There on the pontiff's desk he noticed a gold telephone and was told that this was a direct line to God. When he asked if he might use it he was informed that it would cost him half a million dollars! He decided not to place the call.

On his way home he stopped over in Ireland to trace his roots. When he found the parish from which his ancestors had emigrated he called on the parish priest. As they sat together browsing through the old registers the American noticed a gold telephone on the pastor's desk. Again he was told that it was a direct line to the Lord and when he inquired about the cost of putting a call through the parish priest replied, "It is only tenpence, but be my guest."

"But," stammered the American, "they wanted to charge me half a million dollars in the Vatican!"

"Ah yes," said the pastor, "but you see, over here it's just a local call."

Once I was giving out holy communion in a crowded church. Just as I was about to place the host on a lady's tongue, another person jostled her by wedging into a narrow space beside her. She immediately closed her mouth before receiving, turned to the intruder and called her a bitch, then turned back to me, opened her mouth and said "Amen" to the Body of Christ!

So often we receive the Body of Christ in the Eucharist and fail to recognize it in the pew. So often the tongue that receives the Lord in holy communion is only too ready to lacerate the Body of Christ over a cup of coffee after Mass.

The great French dramatist Jean Anouilh in one of his plays describes heaven as he sees it. The faithful are all gathered with their tickets at the pearly gates. They are assured of admission and are waiting impatiently for the gates to open. On the fringe of the crowd is a small bedraggled group who have no tickets.

A rumor begins to circulate among the chosen ones.

"Did you hear that he's letting them in too?...Well I don't believe it!...After all we did..."

Incredulity gives way to resentment which in turn boils over into anger. Suddenly they begin to shout in protest and to blaspheme God and at that very moment they are all damned.

They were given a last-minute opportunity to recognize the Lord—and they failed.

During the Second World War a little village in Bavaria was virtually wiped out by allied air raids. Among the casualties was the parish church. The figure of Christ on a wayside Calvary beside the church was left without arms and legs. After the war the people set about restoring the church but the parish priest insisted that there be no change or alteration in the wayside shrine. He erected a sign at the foot of the cross which reads: "Now I have no arms and no feet. From now on you will be my arms and feet to bring help and healing to a broken world."

The message is clear. We are to be his arms and feet in the world today. He relies on us to provide each other with strength and support in coping with the many trials and sorrows that inevitably come our way in the course of our lives—the loss of a loved one, loneliness, sickness, and unemployment. When we reach out to others in situations like these we help them to hear the call of Jesus: "Come to me all you who labor and are burdened and I will give you rest." In such moments our support provides an almost tangible presence of the caring compassionate God.

Elie Wiesel recalls a harrowing experience in a Nazi concentration camp. A young boy was sentenced to be hanged in the company of two adults. They mounted the scaffold together and stood on three chairs. As the noose was placed around the neck of the child one of the spectators cried out: "Where is God…where is he?"

The chairs were pulled away and the two adults died instantly. The child was still alive. Here is how Wiesel describes his last moment:

"For more than half an hour he stayed there struggling between life and death and dying in slow agony under our eyes. And we had to look at him full in the face. He was still alive when I passed in front of him. His tongue was still red, his eyes not yet glazed. Behind me I heard the same man asking, "Where is God now?" And I heard a voice within me answer him: "Where is he? Here he is—he is hanging here on the gallows."

6. Light in the Darkness

Your light must shine before people.   *Matthew 5:16*

A few years ago I returned to New Zealand to the scenes of my early ministry. A friend had asked me to look up his sister who lived in Hamilton, a large town in the sheep-farming province of Waikato. I had forgotten her married name; she was just known to me as Peg Hyland. I had even mislaid her address. I told the parish priest with whom I was spending the night about my quest. He had just arrived in the parish but he thought the person I was looking for lived in a particular street. We drove down this long street in the dark and were about to give up when he suddenly brought the car to a halt.

"That must be the place," he said pointing to a house. "It's got to be it! We don't see much of that sort of thing here."

The house to which he pointed was no different from the others except that in this one the blinds in the front room were not drawn and there like a beam we saw a little pin-point of light penetrating the surrounding darkness. It was a little red light illuminating a picture of the Sacred Heart. "Try that one," he said, "and I bet you'll find the one you're looking for!"

He was right. When the door opened to my ring, it was Peg sure enough and her many welcomes 12,000 miles from home were like music to my ears. As we chatted and drank tea from a Tipperary tea-pot it became increasingly clear that the light beneath the picture was the symbol of another light—Christ the Light of the World was a reality in that home. This incident proved to be a useful attention grabber in a talk on family life.

"The Light of the World" is the title of a famous picture painted by Holman Hunt. It shows the thorn-crowned Jesus with a lantern in his hand knocking on a closed door and is based on those lovely words of Christ in Revelation: "Listen, I stand at the door and knock; if anyone hears my voice and opens the door, I will come into his house and eat with him and he will eat with me" (Rev 3:20). The door of course is the human heart and it is said that the artist, having completed the picture, showed it to some friends, who praised the merit of the painting. One of them pointed out what he considered an omission on the part of the artist.

"You have put no handle on the door," he said to Holman Hunt, who replied immediately, "You forget—we must open to the light, the handle is on the inside."

"I am the Light of the World...you are the light of the world," says our Lord. Ours is a derived light, a reflected light just as the moon derives its light form the sun and reflects it.

The English writer John Ruskin has given us a lovely picture of what the Lord wants us to be in our world. In the days before electricity the streets were lit at night by gas-lamps. The lamplighter had to go from lamp to lamp, lighting them with a burning torch. One day Ruskin was sitting in his house looking out a front window. Across the valley was a street on a hillside. There Ruskin could see the torch of the lamplighter lighting lamps as he went. Because of the darkness he could not see the lamplighter, only the torch and the trail of lights it left behind him. After a short while Ruskin turned to the person next to him and said: "There's a good illustration of a Christian. People may never have known him, they may never have met him, they may never even have seen him. But they know he passed through their world by the trail of light he left behind him."

People themselves can be the most effective of all sermon illustrations. All of us can point to people who are and have been lights in the surrounding darkness. One such person was Dr. Brackett. He practiced in a small town in America. He was known as the poor man's friend because of the hours he spent sitting by the bedsides of the less privileged members of the community and the fact that he never took a fee from them. He lived in two rooms over a shop in the middle of the town. At the ground entrance was a brass plate which read: DOC. BRACKETT — OFFICE UPSTAIRS.

At one time in his life he was to have married but the day of the wedding he was called to a poor Mexican family to assist with a difficult childbirth. He stayed with the mother until her child was delivered safe and well. He returned to find that his fiancée had called off the wedding and would have nothing more to do with him. The remainder of his life was one of selfless dedication to the sick, the poor, the old, and the lonely. When he died his funeral was the biggest ever seen.

Then the townspeople came together to discuss ways and means of perpetuating his memory in the town. Various proposals and suggestions were made but as often happens in situations like this nothing was done by anyone except the Mexican couple whose child he delivered on what should have been his wedding day. On the way home from the meeting they removed the sign from his door and the following day it re-appeared over his grave surrounded by flowers. It read: DOC. BRACKETT — OFFICE UPSTAIRS.

6. Light in the Darkness

It was Confirmation time and the bishop asked a boy to describe a saint for him. When the lad showed some hesitancy his lordship pointed to a stained-glass window showing the patronal saint of the parish. The eyes of the young hopeful followed the pointing finger and then reverted to the bishop with a gleam of recognition. "A saint," he said, "is someone who lets the light shine through."

Here are some examples which may prove useful illustrative material.

Terry Fox was a twenty-two-year-old university student in Canada. A keen sportsman, he was on the college basketball team when in 1977 he contracted bone cancer and had to have his right leg amputated. While he was in the hospital, someone sent him a newspaper clipping telling about an amputee who ran in the New York City Marathon.

This fired Terry's imagination so much that he wanted to do something useful with the few remaining years of his life. He decided to run across Canada from the Atlantic to the Pacific to raise money for the fight against cancer. He spent eighteen months practicing running with his artificial leg and then on 12 April 1980 he began to run. He dipped his artificial leg in the Atlantic in Newfoundland and set out with pledges for over one million dollars in his pocket.

Then tragedy struck when he was 114 days and 3,000 miles into the run. The cancer spread to his lungs and he was forced to give up. Like Stephen Roche, he became a hero overnight. As he lay in the hospital pledges totaling twenty-four million dollars came pouring in. When he died, a stamp was issued in his honor and the nation's highest accolade, the Order of Canada, was conferred on him.

But the story does not end there. Donal Marrs, a postman in Cincinnati, decided to complete the run. Like Terry, he too was a cancer victim with just a short time to live. He began in the mid-west and ran to San Francisco. As he dipped his hand in the Pacific Ocean people noticed a large rainbow arched across the sky.

Terry and Donal could have cursed the darkness—instead, they decided to light a candle, as also did a little old man with a sack of acorns in the French Alps.

In 1910 a young explorer was traveling in the French Alps when he came upon a wasteland, a barren stretch of land desolate and abandoned. He had traveled about five miles into this God-forsaken territory when in the distance he saw what looked like the stump of a tree. On approaching, he discovered the stooped figure of a little old man with a sack of acorns on his back and an iron staff in his hand. With the staff he made a hole in the ground, dropped in an acorn and filled the hole. He was planting oak trees. He told the explorer that he had planted 100,000 in the past three years. "If I get one in ten, I'll be happy," he said, adding that his wife and only son had died and that as long as the Lord spared him he would carry on planting trees to bring back life to a land that was dying.

Fifty years later the explorer returned to a sight wondrous to behold. The acorns of 1910 had become an oak forest, eleven kilometers long by three kilometers wide. There were beech trees along the slopes as far as the eye could see. Birds were singing in the trees, wildlife frolicked in the shade and streams flowed with water in groves that had been bone dry. At the entrance to the forest was a linden tree, the symbol of re-birth. And as he gazed in wonder he thought of the old unlettered peasant who had worked alone in utter solitude to turn a desert into the land of Canaan and had completed a task worthy of God.

We may not be able to change the world but we can do something about the little patch where we live. The sack of acorns and the iron staff are in our hands.

Something Beautiful for God is the title given by Malcolm Muggeridge to his biography of Mother Teresa of Calcutta. This tiny, wrinkled, radiant little lady is surely one of the brightest lights in the darkness of today.

Billy Graham, the American evangelist, visited her recently and here is how he describes the experience.

"When I was introduced to her she was ministering to a dying person, holding him in her arms. I waited while she helped him face death. When he died, she prayed quietly, gently lowered him to his bed and turned to greet me.

"We talked till dusk that day. In her lilting broken English she asked if I would like to hear some of her experiences with the hungry and the dying. Very simply she explained her calling to me. Mother Teresa looks past the physical features of every man, woman, and child and sees the face of Jesus staring up at her through them. In every starving child she feeds, she sees Jesus. Around every sick and frightened woman she cares for she sees Jesus. Surrounding every lonely, dying man she cradles in her arms is Jesus. When she ministers to anyone, she is ministering to her Savior and Lord."

"I am the Light of the World!" says the Lord. "You are the light of the world," says the Lord.

How wonderful it would be if we could so live our lives that through us the light of Christ should shine out in the family, out from the family into the street, into the neighborhood, out into the world!

7. The Parables As Jesus Did Not Tell Them

You sometimes wonder if the parables have not been
so historically time-bound—locked away in a
first-century Jewish straitjacket—that Jesus' words have
little obvious reference for us today in this so different
twentieth century.   *A. M. Hunter*

In the first three gospels Jesus tells fifty to sixty stories called
parables. They have been described as heavenly stories with
an earthly meaning or, in the words of P. G. Wodehouse,
"stories in the Bible which sound at first like a pleasant yarn
but keep something up their sleeves which suddenly pops out
and knocks you flat." These stories of Jesus are timeless. Their
message and challenge are for now as truly as they were for
the people who first heard them. They deal with human
existence, with men and women, their joys and sorrows, hopes
and disappointments, successes and failures. Human existence
remains the same but language changes with the passage of
time. The preacher today is faced with the challenge of taking
these timeless stories and applying them to the contemporary
situation in language which will make those who hear them
say, "This concerns me." How a parable can break the shackles
of time and speak its word of God to every age was first
revealed to me during a time when I was religious examiner
of schools in the diocese. It was in a national school in one
of the larger towns which catered to the less academic and
less privileged children of the community.

On my first visit the headmaster drew me aside and asked
me not to stick too closely to the official syllabus as most of

37

his pupils were for export. He added, "We're trying to give them the basics of religion which they can hold onto even in some third-rate lodgings in Birmingham or Manchester." Then he paused, "Ask them the parables," he said. "They like the parables."

Their rendering of the stories of Christ was a revelation. The parables were all up-dated, set in contemporary situations and told in simple and sometimes graphic language. Take, for example, this version of the parable of the Pharisee and Publican: "There were these two lads who went into the chapel to say their prayers. One lad went up to the rails an' lit about six candles and then started braggin' about what a great fella he was.

"'I goes to Mass every morning,' says he, 'and I don't have nothin' to tell in confession because I mind my own business and I don't bother nobody. I'm no sinner, not like him down there.'"

"And who was him down there?" I asked.

"The other fella," he replied, "the lad down at the back of the chapel. He had his head down and wouldn't look up at the altar at all. 'God,' says he, 'I'm a fierce sinner, so please have mercy on my soul.'"

I thought to myself: what better definition of true repentance? Then I asked, "And the message?"

"God listened to the poor ol' devil at the back and he put him back again into the state of grace 'cause he was sorry for what he done an' he wasn't a big bragger like the fella up at the rails."

Some of the parables of Jesus have a way of breaking the shackles of time and speaking their word of God to every age as they did for these young rustic theologians.

One parable of Jesus which escaped the captivity of time and inspired artists like Rembrandt and composers like Debussy is the story of the two sons or, as some have called it, The Story of the Waiting Father. The prodigal son is still with us. He gripes against parental authority or the establishment as he sees it. He wants to get away from it all and have his fling. The elder son is the conventional Christian wrapped up in a world of self-righteousness. T. W. Manson said the younger son wanted an overdraft from his father, the older wanted to open a deposit account, and of the two the latter's is the greater sin. The abiding truth in the story is the kindness of God, the Father, waiting to welcome home the prodigal and to say to the stay-at-home Christian, "Son, you are always with me and all that is mine is yours."

The following stories may help to illustrate how this pearl among the parables can be applied to the contemporary situation.

Take the story of the modern prodigal son who turned up in the "far country" of a neighboring parish. The parish priest advised him to go back home and his father would kill the fatted calf for him. The prodigal did so and some months later he met the parish priest again who asked him hopefully, "Well, and did your father kill the fatted calf for you?"

"No," came the rueful reply, "but he nearly killed the prodigal son!"

This story raises the question: Is this in fact how earthly fathers always welcome home their returning prodigals? Sangster has a version of the story appropriately titled: *The Parable of the Prodigal Son as Jesus didn't tell it.*

"And he arose and set out for his home, and when at last he arrived at the door, he banged and there was no response. He stood there in his piteous rags and hunger for a while, and then he knocked again and a third time; and finally a window opened and his father looked out and said: 'Oh, it's you! You're broke, I suppose. You look a pretty picture. What have you come home for? You've had your share of everything. You know where to come when you're hungry...'

"And he said, 'Father, I have sinned against heaven and in thy sight...' but his father banged the window and left him for a while on the doorstep. Presently his father opened the door and said, 'You're an utter disgrace to me and all your relatives. I'm ashamed of you, utterly ashamed. But I'm your parent, and I've thought it out, and I'm prepared to put you on probation for three months, and if at the end of three months I can find no fault in you, well, perhaps I'll have it in my heart to give you another start...'"

The point is that the story as Jesus *did* tell it is larger than life. The father in the story is not just an ordinary human father but an extraordinary father whose extravagant love knows no bounds.

Some years ago the American Scripture scholar, Barnabas Ahearne, OP, was in Ireland to give an unusual retreat, unusual in the sense that all the participants were members of the Irish hierarchy. Needless to say I was not invited but I did get to hear the lectures which were recorded on tape. Predictably they were all solidly based on Scripture and I was particularly impressed by his modern-day presentation of the parable of the prodigal son. He set it in the context of a bishop's relationship with one of his wayward priests and it went as follows: "Supposing, bishops," he said, "one of your priests creates one hell of a scandal in the diocese; he absconds with diocesan funds and takes himself off to Paris where he lives it up with wine, women...the whole nine yards!

"Then when he's down on his luck, like the prodigal he comes to his senses and says: 'I will arise and go back to Ireland to my father,' and you, bishop, are the only father he's got. What do you do when he comes back to you and tells you that he has sinned against heaven and against you? You run down the steps to meet him, throw your arms around him and then you rent the local hotel and invite all the priests of the diocese to a welcome home dinner!"

"And then," says he, noting the amused reaction of their lordships, "you top it off by making him your vicar general!"

Sister Briege McKenna tells an extraordinary story about a priest in somewhat similar circumstances. Once in the course of a priests' retreat which she was conducting a priest came to her for ministry. As she prayed with him she had a vision of Christ kneeling on a rugged road holding the priest's hands and saying to him, "Robert, forgive yourself, I have forgiven you. Come back to me. Remember the story of the prodigal son. That was you. I'm waiting for you to come back to me. Forgive yourself and return to me again."

When she told him that the Lord had forgiven him he broke down and told her his story. He had been the center of a great scandal which forced him to leave his parish. After a while he acknowledged his mistake but despaired of forgiveness, especially the pardon of his bishop. Then one day after a whole year he read the story of the prodigal son and got the courage to go to his bishop. Here is how he tells the story. "The bishop was sitting at his desk. he got up and came around the desk and took me in his arms. He said like a father to a son, 'Robert, I'll take you back. Jesus has forgiven you, and so do I. But I want you to do one thing. I want you to go to Sister Briege's retreat and I want you to come back to me after the retreat and tell me how you did. I'll place you in a parish.'"

This man like the prodigal son came to his senses and returned to the Lord in repentance. He also experienced the tenderness and fatherhood of his bishop. And Sister Briege's conclusion? "We need to pray that every priest and bishop will have the heart of a father and will discern how to respond in love in any situation."

The following rather unusual allegory comes from South Africa. It was given to me by a good friend who works in a remote mission clinic in the Northern Transvaal. She is Maureen Cahill, a Holy Rosary Sister from Thurles. She called it: The Parable of the Pencil. It can be very effective in teaching and preaching especially if a pencil is used as a visual aid. It has the added merit that it can be used in diverse situations and needs no explanation.

The inventor of the pencil addressed his finished product as follows: "I want you to remember four things:

"First, your goodness or true worth is within you.

"Secondly, you'll need to be sharpened as you go through life.

"Thirdly, you'll be in someone else's hand, otherwise you'll make an awful mess.

"Finally, you'll be expected to leave a mark."

I once used this allegory in a Radio Mass for the sick in the context of human suffering applying the second point to the purifying effect of suffering in our lives. When I returned to the presbytery after Mass the phone was ringing. The caller was from Belfast. "I got the first three points of that parable of the pencil. Could you let me have the fourth one?"

8. God Was There!

So Jesus called a child, made him stand in front of them, and said, "I assure you that unless you change and become like children, you will never enter the Kingdom of Heaven. The greatest in the Kingdom of Heaven is the one who humbles himself and becomes like this child."   *Matthew 18:2-4*

The faith and trust of the secure child are well illustrated in the following story, which has the added merit of being true.

A little boy was admitted to the hospital to have his tonsils removed. He was so nervous and frightened at the prospect of what lay before him that the doctor advised his parents not to come near him until the operation was over. When they did come to visit him they expected to find him upset and distressed, but to their amazement they found him sitting up all excited and eager to tell them of his experience.

"God was there!" he exclaimed. "I saw him and he talked to me."

"Well of course God was there, darling," said his mother, "but you didn't see him and he certainly didn't speak to you."

"He did, he did," the child insisted.

When his father then asked what God looked like, the little lad replied, "He was dressed all in green and I could only see his eyes. He had a green dress and a green cap and a green thing over his mouth."

"I see," said the parent, trying to conceal his amusement, "and how did you know he was God?"

"Well you see, Daddy," came the reply, "there were these three angels around me all dressed in white and two of them were girl angels and the other one was a man angel. The man angel asked me to open my mouth. He looked in and whatever he saw he called to the one in green and said, 'O God come and look at these tonsils.' So God came and looked in and said to me, 'Don't be afraid. I won't hurt you.' So I wasn't a bit afraid because God was doing the job himself!"

As we grow older we tend to lose some of this childlike faith and trust. Take for instance the following story.

The gorge was one thousand feet deep with jagged protruding rocks anchored in its walls. A thin strong wire was tightly stretched across the three-hundred-foot span which separated the two banks. A tense crowd watched and cheered as an acrobat walked the slightly swaying wire.

Then, putting on a blindfold, he walked back along the wire and the crowd cheered even louder. They gasped in astonishment as they saw him cross the gorge again, pushing a wheelbarrow full of sand, with the wire sagging almost to the point of breaking. The moment his feet touched solid ground the terrified people went wild with excitement. One young man threw his arms around him. "You are the greatest," he shouted. "I've never seen anyone like you."

"So you have faith in me?" said the acrobat, emptying the wheelbarrow with a shovel.

"Faith in you?" exclaimed the young man. "I'd depend my life on you."

"Well then," replied the acrobat, "why don't you sit in the wheelbarrow and we'll cross the gorge together?"

The young man's faith immediately evaporated.

Jesus repeatedly demanded faith from his followers, a faith "that staggers not." He told us that if we had faith as small as a mustard seed we too could do marvelous things. If he were the trapeze artist and he asked you to cross the gorge with him, would you have the faith and trust in him to get into the wheelbarrow?

There's another story about a little boy whose five-year-old sister had a rare blood disease and needed a blood transfusion. The blood would would have to come from a relative with the same blood type, and the little boy was suggested as a logical donor.

"Son," said the doctor, "would you give your blood so that your sister can live?" The boy looked shocked but then said he would do it.

The blood was taken and he was still lying in his cot when the doctor came to him and asked how he was feeling.

"Doctor," he asked, "when do I die?"

Only then did it dawn on the doctor that the little boy misunderstood. He thought he had to give *all* his blood to save his sister—just as Jesus gave *all* his blood to save us.

A man looked on in desperation as he saw fire engulfing his house. The flames prevented him from entering. He saw his son in the bedroom window and he yelled, "Jump, son, jump."

In desperation the father called back again, "Jump son. Daddy will catch you."

Trembling with fear the boy stood poised on the window. Then he jumped. He couldn't see; he was frightened out of his wits but he made the leap into his father's arms. He did so because of the faith and trust he had in his father.

Faith is like that—a blind leap into the arms of God.

Christ's regard for children is large in the gospel story. For Christ the child was a living symbol of the kind of character needed for his kingdom. It was not so much the innocence of children as their receptiveness that he had in mind. Unless we are ready to receive God's kingdom as a child takes a present from his parents' hands, we will have no part in it. "Father, Lord of heaven and earth! I thank you because you have shown to the unlearned what you have hidden from the wise and learned" (Mt 11:25).

There's a story from the east about a little boy who lived on the edge of a forest which he had to pass through on his way to and from school. As winter approached he was frightened to go alone so he asked his widowed mother to give him a servant for a companion. Said his mother, "Son, we are too poor to afford a servant. Tell your brother Krishna to accompany you to and from school. He is the Lord of the Jungle. He will surely come with you if you ask him to."

This is just what the little boy did. Next day he called out to his brother Krishna and when Krishna appeared and found out what the boy wanted he agreed to the request.

Then came the schoolmaster's birthday and all the children were expected to bring gifts for the master. The widow said to her son: "We are too poor, son, to afford a gift for your master. Ask your brother Krishna to give you a gift for him." And Krishna did. He gave the boy a jug full of milk, which the boy proudly placed at the feet of the master together with the many other gifts that the other children brought. Then the master said to his servant: "Pour that milk into a basin and return the jug to the boy."

The servant poured the milk into the basin and was going to return the jug when he noticed to his surprise that the jug was full of milk again. Once again he emptied it and once again it filled to the brim. When the master was told he called the boy and asked where he got the jug of milk. "From Brother Krishna," he said.

"Who is he?"

"He is the Lord of the Jungle," said the little boy. "He comes with me to and from school each day."

"Well," said the master in disbelief, "we'd like to see this Krishna you speak of. Take us to him."

The boy went back to the forest followed by the master and all the pupils. When they came to the edge of the forest where the boy met Krishna each day, he called out to him, confident that he would come. But there was no reply. As he kept on calling without response he had to endure the jeers and cat-calls of the pupils and there was a cynical leer on the face of the master.

"Brother Krishna," he called through his tears, "please come. If you do not come they will say I'm a liar. They won't believe me."

There was a moment's silence, then he heard the voice of Krishna saying to him, "Son, I cannot come. The day your master has your purity of heart and your simple childlike faith I shall come."

9. The Devil Takes a Holiday

The Lord asked him "What have you been doing?"
Satan answered, "I have been walking here and there,
roaming round the earth."   *Job 1:7*

This was the title of a book written some years ago in which
the author contends that Satan can now afford to take a
holiday because his allies, the world and the flesh, have
effectively taken over from him. It is even suggested that he
has found himself a new ally in the modern-day preacher who,
if not denying his existence, seldom or ever speaks about him.

True, at baptism we ask the parents and sponsors to
renounce Satan with all his works and empty promises and
the bishop extracts the same promises from the children he
confirms, but do we ever tell the people who the devil is and
what precisely these works and empty promises really are?

It is a far cry from the days when the final prayer of the
Mass scorched itself into our memories:

> Blessed Michael the Archangel
> defend us in the hour of conflict.
> Be our safeguard against the wickedness
> and snares of the Devil.
> May God restrain him we humbly pray,
> and do thou O Prince of the heavenly host
> by the power of God thrust down to hell
> Satan and all other wicked spirits
> who wander through the world
> seeking the ruin of souls.

9. The Devil Takes a Holiday

There's the story of the man who went to a fancy dress ball dressed as the devil. He parked his car and as he ran to the ball venue there was a sudden cloud burst. He ran into a nearby church for shelter and caused instant pandemonium amongst the evening worshipers. In the stampede for the exits hand-bags, rosary beads, and personal belongings were left behind. The hasty departure of one lady came to a sudden halt when her coat got caught in one of the pews. She blurted out in a terrified voice, "Look Satan, I know I've been to Mass every morning for the past twenty years but I want you to know that during all that time I was really on your side!"

Joking apart, when you consider the three temptations Satan set before Christ, she might well have been on his side all those years. The first temptation was to be selfish, to think only of ourselves; the second, to put God to the test, to bargain with God; the third, idolatry, to worship the golden calf of materialism.

Malcom Muggeridge suggests that if the desert encounter took place today there would be a fourth temptation—Christ would be offered primetime on television!

One day the devil was crossing the African desert when he came across a group of small devils who were tempting a holy hermit. They tried him with the seductions of the flesh, all to no avail, then they began to sow doubts and fear in his mind, but the holy man stood firm. As a last resort they surrounded him with creature comforts and told him that his austerities were only a waste of time. But the hermit would not be moved.

Then the devil stepped forward and drew his assistants aside. He told them their methods would never succeed. "Just watch me," he said. Coming up to the hermit he said, "Have you heard the news? Your brother has been made Bishop of Alexandria."

The fable says that on hearing this a scowl of malignant jealousy clouded the serene face of the holy man.

There is a morbid fascination today with Satan and the occult. Demonology confronts us from bookshelves, late night movies and video nasties. *The Exorcist* was one of the most popular movies ever made and the Rolling Stones topped the charts with their "Sympathy for the Devil." Strange, isn't it then, that although Satan was himself a fallen angel and angels are mentioned in the bible more often than demons there are many today, preachers included, who doubt their existence.

I have never once heard a sermon on angels. Come to think of it, I have never preached on the subject myself. Recently a current affairs magazine carried a feature on the new arch-bishop of Dublin under the caption, "On the side of the angels," the implication being one of surprise that an academic could still believe in these heavenly beings.

The devil has had more than his share of attention. It is high time that we turn our minds to the good angels and their influence in the world in which we live. Here is the story of an incident which received wide attention at the time it happened and even found its way into *Readers Digest*.

Dr. W. S. Mitchel, an eminent neurologist from Philadelphia, was in his bed after a long, tiring day when he was aroused from his slumber by the ringing of the door-bell. He made his way downstairs and on the doorstep found a little girl poorly dressed and deeply distressed. She pleaded with him to come to her mother, who was seriously ill. Although it was snowing heavily he decided to follow the child to her home and there he found the mother suffering from a severe attack of pneumonia. He ministered to her and then complimented her on the love and devotion of her child. The woman looked at him strangely and said, "My daughter died a month ago," and then added, "Her shoes and clothes are in the clothes closet there." Dr. Mitchel, amazed and perplexed, opened the closet door. There he found the clothes in which the little girl had appeared to him. They were warm and dry and had not been out that night. Who then came to him on the errand of mercy? Could it have been an angel?

10. Lazarus at the Gate

Our pocket books can have more to do with heaven
and also with hell than our hymn books.

Helmut Thielicke

Pat had just arrived in the New World and was admiring the
sights of New York when he was accosted by a thug who
demanded his money or his life. "Take my life," said Pat. "I
need my money for my old age!"

Once I visited a home in the parish and listened with some
amazement as the couple reminisced about their wedding day. "All we had going to the chapel," the husband said,
"was two pounds. I gave one pound to the priest and seven
shillings and sixpence to the clerk and we set out on our
married life with twelve shillings and sixpence!"

When he saw my look of stunned surprise he smiled and
went on, "But sure we were happy, and we are still happy.
We reared a big family. They're all done for now, thank God!"

Money was scarce in those days but there's an awful lot of
it in circulation now. Thousands of pounds are taken in bank
and post-office raids, and millions are much more skillfully
and painfully extracted from our pockets by the tax collector.

We're all familiar with the stock phrases about money: You
can't take it with you; no pockets in a shroud; the root of all

evil. Actually the last phrase is the one most misquoted. What Paul really said was: The *love* of money is the root of all evil.

Brought up as I was, used to country fairs and markets, I've never been able to fathom the complexities of the stock market. How, for example, can you buy a share in a firm you have never seen from someone who has never seen it either and sell it at a profit to a third person who never intends to visit it, without any of you lifting a finger on the firm's behalf?

I heard of a man whose sole interest in life was playing the stock market. He studied the financial page of the newspaper avidly every day and it became such an obsession with him that one day as he was engrossed in the financial columns he said aloud to himself, "What wouldn't I give to see the paper one year from now!" The words were no sooner out of his mouth than there was a puff of smoke in the room and a genie handed him a newspaper and then disappeared. As soon as he got over the shock he realized that his wish was granted. The paper in his hand was dated one year hence. Feverishly he sought the financial page and his eyes goggled when he saw how the market had developed. He noted the stocks on which he hoped to reap a bonanza. In the bus on his way to visit the stockbroker he was browsing through the rest of the paper when suddenly staring at him from the obituary columns was the notice of his own death and funeral arrangements!

Sometimes preachers fall into the trap of saying that money doesn't matter, that it is of no importance. Of course it matters. It is at the root of most marriage problems. It can never be a pleasant thing to have too little, to not be able to afford the occasional celebration or holiday, to be haunted by insecurity. The question is: Do I possess my possessions or am I possessed by them?

As Christians we must try to find out what Christ had to say about wealth and possessions. For this we must go to the Scriptures. The first thing to emerge is that Christ expects ordinary Christians to live ordinary lives: do their jobs, earn their pay, pay their way and support those who depend on them. This is what Jesus did. Thirty of his thirty-three years on this earth were spent in Nazareth, where he was well-known as the village carpenter. He paid his taxes to the government and to the Temple.

Secondly, he never said that it was a sin to possess money but he does say that it is a grave danger: "Woe to you that are rich.... It is easier for a camel...." To repeat, it is not money but the love of money which is the root of all evil. The danger is always there.

Thirdly, Jesus says that riches are a bad thing in which to place your trust (see the story of the Rich Fool, Lk 12:16-21). They are a very insecure foundation for life. You can't take it with you!

The great English writer Dr. Johnson was once shown around a famous castle and its lovely grounds. He turned to his guide and said, "These are the things that make it difficult to die!"

Fourthly, the desire for money can blind us to higher things—possessions tend to fix our hearts on this world. If we have a large stake in this world it is difficult to think beyond it and especially difficult for us to contemplate leaving it.

Finally, there is the classic story told by Jesus about the Rich Man and Lazarus (Lk 16:19-31). It does not condemn the rich man for being rich but rather for his lack of concern, his lack of awareness of Lazarus. We may well be condemned not for doing something but for doing nothing. Condemnation is for the person who has money and who is quite unaware of those who have not.

10. Lazarus at the Gate

Lazarus is no longer at our gates; television has brought him into our living rooms in those harrowing pictures of starvation in Africa. Contrast this with the food mountains of the European Economic Community (Common Market). This is how the young Albert Schweitzer saw the story of Dives and Lazarus. "We in Europe are Dives," he said. "Out there in Africa lies wretched Lazarus. And just as Dives sinned against Lazarus because, for want of heart, he never put himself in his place and let his conscience tell him what he ought to do, do we sin against the poor at our gate."

11. A Tale of Two Dolls

I am a part of God as the tiniest wave is a part of the
great ocean. What power we have if only we would
plug into the Source of all power!   *Lee Dunne*

Once there was a salt doll who lived so far inland that she
had never seen the sea. Consumed with a desire to see
the sea she set out one day and walked hundreds of miles
toward the ocean. At last she arrived and as she stood on the
sea-shore enraptured by the wonder of what she saw she cried
out, "O Sea, how I would love to know you!"

To her surprise and delight the sea responded to her, "To
know me you must touch me."

So the little salt doll walked toward the sea and as she
advanced into the oncoming tide she saw to her horror that
her toes began to disappear. Then as her feet began to dissolve
she cried out, "O Sea, what are you doing to me?"

The sea replied, "If you desire to know me fully you must
be prepared to give something of yourself."

As the doll advanced further into the water her limbs and
then her body began to disappear and as she became totally
dissolved she cried out, "Now at last, I know the sea!"

The next doll was a creation of love, the love of parents
and grandparents for a little Indian girl of the Comanche
tribe.

11. A Tale of Two Dolls

The greatest drought in living memory brought death and destruction to the Comanches. There was no rain for a year, the land was desolate, people died in the hundreds, and day and night the survivors prayed to the Great Spirit to pity their plight and restore life to the parched earth. One of the few children who survived the disaster was She-Who-Sits-Alone. Her parents and grandparents died in the drought and all that was left to her in the world was her little Comanche doll. It was made by her mother; on its head were the blue feathers of the jay-bird given by her father and the beads on her dress were gathered and put together by her grandparents.

One day she watched the seers of the tribe going up the hill and she spoke to her doll, "The Wise Ones are going up to beg the Great Spirit to send rain."

After many moons the Wise Ones returned and told the awaiting people that the Great Spirit had spoken and complained that the people had grown selfish; that they had taken from the earth more than they had ever put into it; that if there was to be an end to the drought then each person must be prepared to give up his/her most valuable possession as a burnt offering. The ashes were to be scattered to the four winds and then the Great Spirit would send rain and the earth would yield its fruits.

The people thanked the Great Spirit and went back to their tents to reflect on their most valuable possessions and the sacrifices they were asked to make. One said, "Surely the Great Spirit does not expect me to give up my horse!" Another said, "The Great Spirit would not expect me to yield my gun," and another, "How could I be expected to sacrifice my bow?" Selfishness took over and they could not persuade themselves to part with their most prized possessions.

Then She-Who-Sits-Alone spoke to her doll, "It looks as if you're the one the Great Spirit wants. You are my most valuable possession, given to me by my parents and grandparents."

That night when all were asleep the little girl left her tent, lit a torch from the campfire and clasping her doll climbed to the top of the hill where the Great Spirit had spoken to the

Wise Ones. She collected a bundle of sticks, lit them with the torch and then, grief-stricken, hugged her doll. Then remembering the words of the Great Spirit she lovingly placed the doll in the fire. Tears flooded her eyes as she watched it disappear in the flames. Gathering the ashes she turned to the four winds of heaven and scattered them on the hilltop. Then she lay down on the barren earth and went to sleep with a smile on her lips.

She awoke in the morning to the touch of a gentle breeze on her face and in her hair and she gazed in wonder at a sea of blue not merely in the sky but all over the hill and down into the plain. The earth was covered with beautiful blue flowers as far as the eye could see.

The people emerging from their tents were transfixed by the beautiful scene. They ran to the hilltop and as they did the rain began to fall and then they realized what She-Who-Sits-Alone had surrendered to the Great Spirit. They sang and danced for joy and henceforth called the little girl: She-Who-Loved-Her-People. To this day the Comanches will tell you how every spring the Great Spirit, remembering the love of the little girl, sends gentle rain from heaven and covers hill and dale with beautiful blue flowers.

12. Father John—Storyteller Supreme

Preaching is the minister's effort to answer on Sundays
the questions his people have been asking him in the
week.   *William E. Sangster*

Pastoral contact with people is a rich source of sermon
illustration. The preacher who is in touch with the people,
who meets them in their homes, places of work, and recrea-
tion, sees and hears things that have valuable homiletic use.
In my experience the master craftsman in this respect was
Canon John Hayes of Bansha, or Father John as he was
affectionately known to thousands all over Ireland and especially to the people of his native diocese and parish.

Father John was a visionary in more sense than one, who
spoke and preached in pictures. Today's theologians lay
special emphasis on the personal witness of the preacher.
Edward Schillibeeckx writes: "We do not merely toss out
dogmas to men who are crying out in dire need. We begin to
teach Christian truth successfully by ourselves beginning to
live for our fellow men. Our life must itself be the incarnation
of what we believe, for only when dogmas are lived do they
have any attractive power."

John Hayes was a preacher whose life gave credible witness
to his words. His transparent humanity ensured that the good
news he preached was listened to and believed. His homilies
were loaded with the realities of the human heart, the plight
of the poor and unemployed on his doorstep, and the univer-
sal questions of love and hate, pain and hope, joy and grief,
life and death. Unlike this writer he never had to borrow other
people's stories. They were all his own, told in his own
inimitable style, and derived from a wealth of pastoral expe-

rience. *There is nothing that illustrates life like life* was one of his maxims, and almost all of his illustrations were taken from real life. I first heard him as a student in Maynooth when he came to speak to us on Muintir na Tire, the great Christian rural movement which he founded. He had us thinking furiously half the time and laughing uproariously for the remainder.

Perhaps I should make it clear at the outset that some of the following stories and anecdotes could hardly be regarded as illustrative sermon material but they do provide a valuable insight into a man who was a gifted preacher and born storyteller.

He used to tell one of his classic stories to illustrate the fact that all even the most irreligious Irishman needs is a little spirituous refreshment to develop an interest in the things of the spirit.

Late one night Father John was roused from his slumbers by the incessant ringing of the doorbell punctuated by a hail of pebbles peppering the bedroom window. Opening the window he recognized one of his parishioners looking up at him, very agitated and unsteady on his feet from drink.

"Come down and talk to me, Father," came the plea from below, "I can't sleep a wink all night thinkin' of the *skisims* in the church!"

"Bill," said Father John, "do you realize what hour of the night it is?"

"I do, Father, and I'm sorry to be throublin' you, but them *skisims* have me driven to disthraction!"

"All right, Bill, why can't you come back in the morning when you're sober and we'll talk about the schism?"

"But sure Father, when I'm sober, I don't give a bloody curse about the *skisims!*"

I heard him tell a story about one of his parishioners who had a magnificent shroud against the day of his departure. It was handmade and embroidered with loving care by his sister, a nun. Every day he'd take it out and admire it and sometimes he'd even put it on, as he said, "I wanted to see how I'd look when they lay me out. I came into the world a bit rough as one of eight children. Now I'm making sure I'll go out respectable!"

Well, one of his neighbors died rather suddenly and the family, wishing to wake him "decent," besought Pakie for a loan of the shroud, giving him a solemn assurance that it would be returned to him dry-cleaned before the funeral. After a lot of hummin' and hawin' he reluctantly agreed. The wake was a triumph; the general consensus was that the shroud took years off the corpse—in fact he looked so well in it that they didn't have the heart to take it off him. And so in spite of all their promises they buried him in it and sent Pakie a rather shoddy habit as a replacement.

When Father John got wind of it, he called on Pakie and, feigning ignorance, asked for a look at the famous shroud.

"Take a look at it," said Pakie in disgust as he produced the substitute garment.

"Glory be to God, Pakie, surely you're not going to be seen dead in that."

"I'm not," said Pakie, bundling the habit into a ball and throwing it in the corner.

"I'm going to go before me God in me shirt!"

He was an obvious target for hard luck stories and one day when out for a stroll he was accosted by two of his regular clients—a husband and wife. The man was in his bare feet and when Father John expressed concern the wife spoke up, "Yerra Lord Canon, didn't our poor Lord have to go 'round in his bare feet, didn't he climb up that hill with the cross an' he in his bare feet, didn't they drive the nails through his poor feet, didn't they?"

Deeply impressed by this manifestation of faith, Father John was about to give his customary "God bless you" when the woman sighed, "but sure the Canon alanna, if he had the price of a pair of boots sure he wouldn't have to put up with all that hardship, would he?"

On another occasion he was commending a lady for her heroic fortitude in suffering and adversity and he assured her that a special crown awaited her in the next life. "Well, the way things are with me now," she replied, "I'd gladly settle for half-a-crown in this life!"

Once he was confronted with the problem of predestination in, of all places, a hay meadow. The hay was being saved so he went in to say, "God bless the work."

"See here, Canon," said the farmer leaning on his fork, "will you answer me one question that's been bothering me for some time. Tell me now, doesn't God know everything?"

"Sure he does," came the reply.

"Doesn't he know that I'm going to be saved or I'm going to be lost?"

"Hmmm. I suppose he does."

"Then tell me why should I be bothering trying to save my soul. I'm not going to change his mind for him. Am I?"

"Well now, Bill," said Father John after a little thought, "we're agreed that the good Lord knows everything—aren't we?"

"Sure, Canon."

"Doesn't he know that this crop of hay will be saved or lost, doesn't he?"

"I suppose he does, right enough!"

"Well then, Bill, why don't you get up on your tractor and go home: You're not going to change his mind are you?"

The farmer looked at him, got the message and went back to saving the hay.

Stephen Rynne in his biography of Father Hayes tells a story about an old woman who made her living by selling fruit on the street and who was over-fond of the bottle. One day with a basket of oranges on her head and very much the worse for drink she met Father Hayes. Calling down blessings on him she began bobbing up and down in half-genuflections. Every time she bobbed, a few oranges bounced out of the basket. Father Hayes ran around picking them up for her, until he got tired of it. Finally he handed her a few shillings, "Here you are, Mam. You'd better have another drink to steady yourself."

Father John's name is inseparably linked with Muintir na Tire but there was another aspect of his apostolate perhaps less well-known but nevertheless one to which he was deeply committed. That was the work of the Catholic Evidence Guild. For many years he was a soap-box orator in Hyde Park, where he held audiences spell-bound with his crystal clear exposition of Catholic teaching garnished with good humor and of course the inevitable story. He enjoyed being heckled and if there was a facetious question then the inquirer could expect a reply in kind. Like the time he turned the tables on a joker who heckled him, "Why does your Church lock up all those beautiful young girls in convents?" to which came the quick response, "Well first of all let me assure you that they are not all beautiful, and secondly we don't lock them in...we lock guys like you out!"

On one occasion he was almost floored by a question on an historical issue. A lady asked him what was the Catholic position regarding the Casket Letters. He had never heard of the Casket Letters but to show ignorance before a crowd of five hundred would be fatal so he deftly turned the issue back to the questioner. "Lady," says he, "as you will know there are at least two conflicting opinions on these Letters. Which, may I ask, do you hold?" Only too pleased to air her views she took the bait and in so doing gave him some idea of what it was all about. Then he proceeded to give her back her own view, slightly embellished, of course. Afterward she approached him and thanked him for the most lucid explanation of the problem that she had yet received!

He used to wryly reminisce about another occasion when he felt that he might have let down the cause. This time he found himself in the role of heckler. On the soap box was an Ulster Orangeman explaining why Ulster would never bend the knee to a Popish state. He then went on to attack the primacy and infallibility of the pope. Throughout the harangue John Hayes kept heckling him, eventually challenging him to hand the soap-box over to him for a rebuttal. To his astonishment the Orangeman accepted the challenge and invited him on to the platform. As Father John told it afterward, "I felt that in courtesy I should thank him for giving me the stage, then I went on to acknowledge his sincerity and to admit the few points where he could have been right. I was just about to take him to pieces when the police blew their whistles to mark the end of all public speaking in the park. I got down from the platform with my tail between my legs and was walking away dispiritedly when I got a tap on the shoulder. Looking around there was the Orangeman, soap-box under one arm, the other hand outstretched. "Put it there mon," says he. "You'll be one of us yet!"

Another great raconteur was Father Maurice Browne, author of *The Big Sycamore*. A Tipperary man born and raised at the foot of Slievenamon, he had some wonderful flights of the imagination. His stories, humorous and gripping in themselves, could also be severely utilitarian, for example the one he used tell about an old priest's dream which cured the parishioners for a long time of being late for Mass.

One Sunday when the parish priest was reading the gospel there was a constant din of feet coming up the aisle. Father Phil paused for a while and then told the congregation about his dream the previous night. "I dreamt that I was present at the Day of Judgment. The entire human race from Adam down to the last-born was assembled in the Valley of Jehosaphat. The crowd stretched for miles and miles as far as the eye could see. It was like a vast cornfield waiting for the reaper. The Judge was sitting on his throne surrounded by all the angels and saints. The books were opened but there was a delay in starting the judgment. The suspense was terrible as the people waited. Then away on the far horizon a small cloud could be seen drifting nearer and nearer. It stopped on the outskirts of the vast assembly. The Judge turned to the Angel Gabriel and said, "Let the Judgment begin. They have come in from the parish of Ballyknock!"

13. The Beggar on the Rock

In the evening of life we shall be judged on love.
St. John of the Cross

An ancient cross on the Rock of Cashel marks the spot where St. Patrick baptized King Aengus. According to the legend, as he stood by the throne and addressed the assembled people he inadvertently pierced the king's foot with his crozier. Later, when to his horror he saw the royal blood flowing on the ground, he exclaimed to the monarch, "Why didn't you cry out?" to which the king replied, "I thought this was to be my share in the suffering of Christ!"

According to another legend Aengus became a very saintly and exemplary ruler, but like many a monarch he was beset by one abiding problem—he had no children to succeed him. The story goes that he sent messengers to every village and town to post notices seeking eligible young men to come to him for interview with a view to the succession. There were just two qualifications: the candidate must have a great love of God and of neighbor. A young man in one of the villages saw the notice. He was a committed Christian who would qualify on both counts. An inner voice told him that he should apply for an interview, but he too had a problem. He was very poor and had no decent clothes to wear before the king. He decided to beg for money to buy clothes and food for the long journey to Cashel. At length when he collected enough to purchase apparel and food for the return journey he set out on the long trek to the king's palace on the Rock. After many days traveling he saw the king's castle on the huge granite rock in the center of the Golden Vale of Tipperary, and as he approached the Rock he noticed a beggar dressed in rags

67

sitting by the wayside. As he passed, the beggar pleaded with him, "I am cold and hungry. Please give me some clothes and food or I will die." The young man's heart went out to the beggar so he gave away his costly apparel and put on the tattered coat of the beggar. He also gave him half of his food and then hesitantly made his way to the Rock. The palace attendants gave him anything but reassuring looks as they ushered him into a waiting room. After a long wait he was summoned up to the king's presence. He bowed low and when he looked up he gasped in astonishment.

"You were the beggarman I met!"

When the king nodded he asked, "Why did you do it?"

"I had to be sure that you really did love God in your neighbor," the king replied.

So much for the legend but the point it makes is exactly the same as that contained in Christ's dramatic account of the Last Judgment in Matthew 25:31-46. At the end of our lives we will be judged on how well we served Christ in the least of our brothers and sisters.

I like the story of the man who had to face the Lord in judgment. As he took his place in the queue he took no comfort from the judgments he heard being handed out. To one person the Lord said, "Enter...because I was hungry and you gave me to eat"; to another, "Come...I was a stranger, and you took me in"; to a third, "I was sick and you visited me." Our friend got more and more dejected as he heard the Lord meting out rewards for the corporal works of mercy because he couldn't see himself qualifying on those grounds.

Then it came to his turn and the Lord looked at him kindly and said: "Like you I was once dejected and downcast and you told me funny stories; I was depressed and you made me laugh. Come you blessed!"

It was Munster Final Day in Thurles. What's more it was Centenary Year and the atmosphere was electric as thousands of Cork supporters converged on the town from an early hour, sporting the red and white colors of the Rebel County.

In an effort to offer the eleven o'clock Mass I had to run the gauntlet of a solid phalanx of Corkonians camped on the Cathedral steps. As I tried to make my way through them I became the target of a lot of good-humored banter: "Don't forget to say one for us, Father. Yerra don't bother Father. We'll bate ye fair!"

When I faced the congregation the sight was awesome. The seats were strewn with red and white caps and draped with red and white flags. There were easily two thousand in the church and loudspeakers relayed the service to the hundreds of sun-worshipers outside. All minds were preoccupied with Semple Stadium. As an attention grabber I tried a story on them which was perhaps relevant to the occasion but certainly not to the message. The critics may not approve but it seemed right at the time!

The story tells of how Glen Rovers were playing old rivals, St. Finbarrs, in the Cork County Final. The Barrs snatched victory from the jaws of defeat when their full-forward scored a hotly disputed goal in the last minute. The Glen backs protested to no avail that he was in the square at the time. Finbarrs' celebrations went far into the night and ended in tragedy when the player who scored the controversial goal lost his life in a car accident in the early hours of the morning.

The scene now shifts to the Judgment Hall where our friend, escorted by an angel, is awaiting his turn to face the Heavenly Tribunal. He confides his worry about the goal to the angel. He feels now that he might have been in the square and if so that the goal should be disallowed. The angel does nothing to reassure him, pointing out that the heavenly powers take a dim view of anything that savors of dishonesty, of taking credit where it was not due. The angel then left him for a while and he sat alone feeling miserable until a little saint whom he did not recognize came over and sat beside him. He told his worries to the saint and to his delight got the reassurance he needed. The little saint told him that he himself happened to be watching the match the previous day, that he had an excellent view and that there was do doubt whatsoever about St. Finbarrs' win as the goal was perfectly legitimate. The forward was cheered no end as the saint left him.

The angel returned to escort him to the Judgment and the Barrs' man confidently assured him that his fears had vanished because he had it on reliable authority that the goal was perfectly fair!

"Whose authority, might I ask?" said the angel.

"That little saint waving at me over there!"

"Yerra don't mind him," said the angel, "that fellow is biased. That's *St. Finbarr!*"

I was in prison, and you visited me."
Lord, what you ask is hard. It's not so easy to visit you these days, especially when you find yourself in an Irish prison. Remember last year, Lord, when you sent word to me that you'd like me to come and see you in prison. Well I did come, but I wonder did you realize all the hassle I had to undergo to spend those few minutes with you. I knew from the beginning that it wouldn't be easy but I wasn't prepared for anything like this.

First of all I called them up and told them that I was a priest and that you wished to see me. I told them that I would come during normal visiting hours so as not to interfere with prison routine or usurp the duties of the prison chaplain, although, as you know I was a prison chaplain myself for many years and met you often then without hindrance, but then that was in another country where they weren't quite so security conscious! Well anyway, they hummed and they hawed and passed me from one official to another before finally giving a grudging assent.

Chastened by this experience I set out for the prison. After a brief and courteous interrogation by a guard, I was directed through some wire meshing to a wooden hut to be further interrogated by two prison officers. I explained that I was a priest and that my visit was purely a pastoral one and I showed them my passport as identification. They directed me to another room where I was told to empty my pockets before being body searched. They kept my car keys in case I'd try to spring you. Then I was taken to yet another room to await my turn to pass through the prison gates. Finally the summons came and I passed through two sets of prison gates to a room in the main building where I saw a long line of prisoners seated side by side and talking over a wooden barrier to their visitors under the supervision of prison officers. Then I saw you in the midst of them.

Sandwiched between two other visitors I tried to talk to you but the din was so great I could only hear you with difficulty. Then it was time to go. The guards stirred uneasily as I reached over the barrier to place my hand on your head in blessing. Then I left you. Getting out was much easier. Anyway Lord, I did try!

But then again, Lord, maybe you had other prisons in mind besides those with iron bars and strip searches. Were you by any chance thinking of all those in my parish and community who are locked away in the cells of loneliness and depression? Are you perhaps pointing an accusing finger at me and telling me that I locked them in with my coldness and indifference?

We seldom see you hungry these days, Lord, at least not here in Ireland, but then you did suggest another type of hunger when you said, "Man cannot live on bread alone but needs every word that God speaks" (Mt 4:4). How do I break the bread of your word with your people? What am I doing about the hungry sheep who look up and are not fed?

Have I ever seen you thirsty, Lord? Remember the man who came to me in the sacristy one morning after Mass. He had unique talents which he wanted to put at the disposal of the parish. He was thirsty for recognition and I gave him the cold shoulder. Was that you, Lord?

Never in my nice country parish have I seen you homeless, Lord. But then maybe you are. What about those rendered homeless by grief and bereavement, those whose home has through the loss of a loved one suddenly become just four walls, those who live with their memories and wait for me just to sit down and listen?

Of course I've never seen you naked, but on second thought perhaps I have. Remember that woman, Lord, whose son brought shame and dishonor on the family and who was tortured by what the neighbors "might be saying" about her? She was naked, Lord. All she needed was to be clothed in the garments of my comfort and compassion.

When did I see you a stranger, Lord? What about the coldness in my parish? What have I done to integrate new-comers and make them feel welcome in the community?

As I re-read your dramatic words about the last Judgment in Matthew I recall some of the words from a poem by Brewer Mattocks. It goes like this:

> The parish priest of Austerity
> Climbed up in a high church steeple
> To be nearer God
> So that he might hand
> His word down to his people
> And he cried from the steeple
> "Where art thou Lord?"
> And the Lord replied,
> "Down here among my people."

14. Having a Go at the Clergy

Working for the Lord may not pay well, but the
retirement benefits are out of this world.   *Anonymous*

Once at a wedding reception, I was sitting in the hotel
lounge, awaiting the summons to the dining room, when
I noticed one of my parishioners eyeing me rather unsteadily
from the public bar. Next thing he was over to me, pint in one
hand, the other outstretched. "Lave it there, Father," says he,
"I always stand up for you in the pubs."

And then as he downed the pint he let me in on a few of
the things that "they (this ubiquitous 'they') do be saying about
ye."

Criticizing the clergy is a time-honored pastime. Having
listened to my friend I am convinced that men are capable of
doing a far more effective hatchet job over a pint than the
much maligned ladies over a cup of morning coffee. Be that
as it may, to quote the *seanchai,* there was a time when I was
quite sensitive to criticism but I've gotten over that phase,
thank God. Now, I think I'd be more worried if "they" weren't
talking about us, as that would be a sign that they were no
longer interested in us.

A parish priest was once subjected to a barrage of criticism
over the lack of activity in his parish. Time and again he
heard the complaint that the parish was dead. Then one

Sunday when reading the obituary list he announced to a startled congregation that he regretted to have to inform them that the parish was dead and that he would be conducting a full funeral service the following Sunday.

Needless to say during the week a lot of froth was blown off the pints and the coffee cups clinked as speculation grew over the forthcoming obsequies. The following Sunday a packed congregation was confronted by the sight of an open coffin in front of the altar. The priest preached a touching homily on the demise of the parish and then, after the final commendation and farewell, he invited the congregation to come up in single file to pay their last respects. Of course the coffin was empty but unknown to them the priest had placed a full length mirror along the bottom board.

Then as the people looked in what they saw staring up at them was their own faces!

Then there was the parish priest who was seriously ill in the hospital and was visited by the chairman of the parish council. "Father, we want you to keep up your heart and not to worry. At our meeting last night we voted eight to two to pray for your recovery!"

"You never came to see me when I was in the hospital. I could have been dead and buried for all the clergy knew or cared!" Complaints like these, not unfamiliar to all of us, probably inspired the following lines:

> The doctor went to see him
> But the pastor didn't go.
> The doctor—he was sent for.
> But the pastor didn't know.
> The doctor was rewarded
> with a handsome little check,

But the pastor, for not knowing,
Simply got it in the neck!

"Ah sure you don't need any prayers, Father!" One of the commonest misconceptions amongst the laity is that priests don't need their prayers, that we've got it made, God help us. How seldom do priests' names figure in the anniversary lists read out every Sunday. I once remarked on this in clerical company, adding, "I'm convinced that there is nothing more dead than a dead priest." At the time I was within earshot of the bishop who came out with the wry comment, "There is—a dead bishop!"

Priests are obvious targets for hard-up stories leading inevitably to hand-outs. The needy and the not-so-needy accost us on the streets, on the presbytery door-step, outside the church after Mass. They know where and when to find us. I suppose we should be flattered but often our reaction is one of annoyance. We distinguish between the deserving and undeserving poor; we expect the housekeeper to provide a protective screen for us. I am sure that many, particularly knights of the road, have memories of priests who were kind to them and so they keep coming back despite rebuffs.

Canon John Hayes of Bansha had so many callers that his presbytery was facetiously known as Hayes's Hotel. His brother Mick used to often recall how one day when he was staying at the presbytery, "We said we'd count them, just for one day. I think 'twas a 112 we made it, that's postman and all!"

14. Having a Go at the Clergy

John Stott tells the story of a country vicar to whom a homeless woman turned for help, and who (doubtless sincerely, and because he was busy and felt helpless) promised to pray for her. She later wrote this poem and handed it in to a regional office of *Shelter!*

I was hungry,
    and you formed a humanities group to
    discuss my hunger.
I was imprisoned,
    and you crept off quietly to your chapel and
    prayed for my release.
I was naked,
    and in your mind you debated the morality
    of my appearance.
I was sick,
    and you knelt and thanked God for your
    health.
I was homeless,
    and you preached to me of the spiritual
    shelter of the love of God.
I was lonely,
    and you left me alone to pray for me.
You seem so holy, so close to God.
    But I am still very hungry—and lonely—and
    cold.

There is an obvious pit-fall here for us priests. How often do I tell people I'll pray for them, when I myself am the prayer they need.

The following rather hackneyed piece by an anonymous author contains a modicum of truth insofar as it shows the no-win situations in which priests sometimes find themselves:

> If his sermon is a few minutes longer than usual, "He wears you out."
> If it's short, "He hasn't bothered."
> If he raises his voice, "He deafens you."
> If he speaks normally, "You can't hear one word he says."
> If he's away, "He's always on the road."
> If he stays at home, "He's a stick-in-the-mud."
> If he's out visiting, "He's never at home."
> If he's in the presbytery, "He never visits his people."
> If he talks finances, "He's too fond of money."
> If he doesn't, "No one knows what he's up to."
> If he organizes functions, "He's stuck in too many things."
> If he doesn't, "The parish is dead."
> If he takes time in the confessional, "He's too inquisitive."
> If he doesn't, "He never listens."
> If he starts Mass on time, "His watch must be fast."
> If he starts a minute late, "He's never on time."
> If he is young, "He lacks experience."
> If he is old, "He ought to retire."
> And if he dies, "Sure of course, no one could ever take his place."

Never mind! The story could be worse. It could happen to a bishop!

If we do take it upon ourselves to preach the occasional sermon on priest-bashing, we might well consider the possibility that those who talk about us in the pubs and over the tea-cups may well have legitimate grievances. Many of those who listen to us on Sunday are people who have been hurt by the institutional church. Women in particular see themselves as second-class citizens with little or no role to play in the life of the community. Then there is the coldness of some parishes, the caste system which looks askance at the "blow-in." A priest was walking around the church during Sunday Mass when he noticed a man wearing a hat. He asked for an explanation and received the following reply, "I've been in your parish for one year now and I felt I had to do something to attract your attention."

Money, possessions, vacations, and general life-style can be areas of irresponsibility in our lives which attract unwelcome criticism. This is true of money, in particular—the frequency with which it is spoken about, the way it is collected, the way it is spent, and the lack of accountability for it. We spend a lot of our priesthood persuading people that they do not have a gripe, but so often they are able to prove us wrong.

Despite the Second Vatican Council's redefinition of the laity as the whole people of God and the Synod of Bishops which was expressly summoned to discuss the mission of the laity, the lay voice is still not adequately heard in the church. We still see laypeople as recipients of church services or helpers on the fringes of clerical ranks. We've drawn them into the Sunday morning church as lay ministers rather than send them out with a sense of mission to the Monday church of the market-place.

But that's another story for another storyteller!

15. He's Always Looking for Money

Give until you feel it, and then keep on giving until
you don't feel it.   *D. L. Moody*

In the whole range of pastoral activity the most difficult task facing the priest is the quest for money. There is no topic better calculated to raise the people's ire and get their backs up than the constant emphasis on finance.

I heard of a priest who had a special flair for holding collections on the slightest pretext. One Sunday toward the end of Lent his congregation was startled when they heard him announce a special collection to defray the cost of the palms for Passion Sunday. Sensing their stunned reaction he added, by way of justification, "Palms don't grow on trees, you know!"

I like the approach of one preacher who found himself literally weighed down every Monday morning by the load of tenpence coins he had to carry to the bank. One Sunday he told his people the story of the tenpence coin and the pound that left the treasury on the same day and met one year later in the cash-box of a supermarket. The pound narrated all the experiences it had over the twelve months. It had been to the races, the pictures, bingo, the pub and to football matches. The tenpence listened rather enviously and then commented, "Well I hadn't nearly as exciting a time, but I can tell you one thing: I never miss Mass on Sundays!"

A variation of the above story goes like this:

The tenpence coin tells its story: "I'm only tenpence, a very small coin. I am not on speaking terms with the butcher. I'm much too small to buy a glass of beer or even a bar of chocolate. I'm not big enough to purchase an ice-cream or a

Sunday newspaper. A permanent wave won't look at me. They won't let me in to bingo or the disco. I'm not even fit for a tip. But believe me, when I go to Mass on Sunday, I'm considered some money!"

A little boy observed his mother putting tenpence in the offering plate at Mass. On the way home he heard her cutting the sermon to pieces. "But mother," said he, "what more could you expect for tenpence?"

The story is told of a farmer who was known for his generous giving and people noticed that the more he gave the more he prospered. One day someone mentioned this to him and asked him how it was. The farmer thought for a while then said, "I keep shoveling into God's bin and God keeps shoveling back into mine and God must have the bigger shovel."

Maurice Browne has a classic story about a priest who found it hard to collect his dues. He made a pilgrimage to Rome and was so impressed by what he saw that he decided to give an account of it in the pulpit the following Sunday. He began by telling them about the papal audience and how the pope picked him out of all those present.

"Tell me, my good man," said the pope, "where do you come from?"

"From Ireland, Your Holiness."

"From what part of Ireland?"

"From Gurteen, Your Holiness."

The pope looked slightly non-plussed.

"Are the people of Gurteen devoted to the church?"

"The best in the world, Your Holiness."

"Do they attend Mass regularly?"

"Every Sunday in winter and summer they come to Mass from the farthest ends of the parish, from over the hills and out of the bogs. Not an hour of the day but you'd see them making visits, and every evening they say the rosary in their homes."

"Tell me, Father," said he then, "do they pay their dues?"

"And there, my dear people," said the priest from the pulpit, "I had to hold down my head."

"O, Father! Father," said His Holiness, "I never expected that from the people of Gurteen!"

There was a substantial increase in collections!

16. The Richest Man in the Valley

Make your vision apparent by shock—to the hard of hearing you shout, and for the almost-blind you draw large and startling figures.   *Flannery O'Connor*

This classic story by Harold Wildish illustrates the folly of placing our entire trust in earthly values.

There was a wealthy laird who lived in the Scottish Highlands. He was more than richly endowed with the world's goods and amongst his vast possessions was a stately mansion overlooking a beautiful valley. But there was a basic emptiness in his life. He had no religious belief, and he lived alone, possessed by his possessions.

In the gate lodge at the entrance to his estate lived John, his herdsman. John was a man of simple faith and deep religious commitment. With his family he was a regular church-goer, the Lord's presence was a reality in his home, and often at night when he opened the gate to admit his employer the laird noticed the family on their knees in prayer.

One morning the laird was looking out on the valley resplendent in the rising sun. As he gazed on the beautiful scene he was saying to himself, "It is all mine," when he heard the doorbell ringing. Going down he found John on the door step. "What's the matter, John?" he asked. "Are the horses all right?"

John looked embarrassed. "Yes sir," he replied. "Sir, could I have a word with you?" He was invited in on to the plush carpet, a striking contrast between their life-styles.

"Sir," said John hesitantly, "last night I had a dream, and in it the Lord told me that the richest man in the valley would die tonight at midnight. I felt I should tell you. I hope, sir, you don't mind."

"Tut, tut," said the laird. "I don't believe in dreams. Go on back to your work and forget about it."

John still looked uneasy. "The dream was very vivid, sir, and the message was that the richest man in the valley would die at midnight tonight. I just had to come to you, sir, as I felt you should know."

The laird dismissed him, but John's words that the richest man in the valley would die at midnight kept bothering him, so much so that at eleven o'clock that morning he took out his car and went to the local doctor for a complete check-up. The doctor examined him, pronounced him fit as a fiddle and said he'd give him another twenty years. The laird was relieved but a lingering doubt caused him to invite the doctor around for dinner and a few drinks that evening. They enjoyed a sumptuous meal together and shortly after eleven-thirty the doctor got up to leave, but the laird prevailed on him to remain on for a few night-caps.

Eventually, when midnight passed and he was still in the land of the living, he saw the doctor to the door and then went up the stairs muttering, "Silly old John...upset my whole day...him and his damned dreams!"

No sooner was he in bed when he heard the doorbell ringing. It was twelve-thirty. Going down he found a grief-stricken girl at the door, whom he recognized instantly as John's teenage daughter.

"Sir," she said looking at him through her tears, "Mammy sent me to tell you that Daddy died at midnight."

The laird froze as it was suddenly made clear to him who was the richest man in the valley.

There was once a rich lady who lived on her own and led an impeccable life as far as the externals of religion were concerned. She went to Mass daily and found little or nothing to confess when she went to confession because, as she repeatedly asserted, she "never bothered anybody."

Eventually she died and to her horror and surprise found that she had been assigned to hell. She went to the devil and complained bitterly about her treatment, explaining how she had lived a virtuous and utterly blameless life on earth and claiming that the powers up above must surely have made a mistake.

Satan, being in a benevolent mood, said he'd look into her case and straight away got on the hot-line to St. Peter, who immediately assured him that there was no mistake, that the good lady was sent to where she properly belonged. Peter then added, "She's the most selfish and self-centered person we've ever yet come across. She's never parted with anything in her life. She does not know what it is to give. If she'd given even a penny to someone in need we'd have taken her in."

"Supposing," said Satan, "that she had performed just one charitable deed in her lifetime, would you accept her?" to which Peter replied, "Certainly." Then the devil explained the situation to the lady, advising her to do some soul searching in the assurance that if she discovered even one charitable act in her lifetime that heaven would be open to her.

After a few days of self-examination she returned to Satan in high spirits, saying that she could recall one good deed which she had done. "One day," said she, "as I was cooking the dinner a beggar-man came to the back door. He was hungry, so I gave him an onion."

The devil relayed her story to Peter, who checked out the incident and then got back to Satan saying, "Yes, it's true. She did give an onion away on just that one occasion. As a matter of fact we have the onion. It was such a rare occurrence that we had it displayed in the museum up here."

"Does that mean," asked the devil, "that you are still prepared to accept her up there?"

"It does," replied Peter, "this is what we'll do. We are going to lower the onion into your department at the end of a rope. Tell her to clasp it and then we'll pull her up here."

Needless to say the lady was overjoyed as the rope was lowered with her onion dangling on the end of it. She grabbed the onion and suddenly her feet left the nether region. As she was being pulled up, some of her companions, seeing an opportunity of getting out with her, clung to her.

"Let go, let go," she shrieked, kicking out at them, "that's my onion."

With the words, "That's my onion," the rope snapped and she fell back, with her onion, into the arms of Satan, who said to her, "The rope was strong enough to save both you and your brothers, but it was not strong enough to save you alone."

This story would tend to bear out the following description of a self-centered lady: Johanna lived in a little world bounded north, south, east, and west by...Johanna!

Its message is somewhat similar to that of the vision of hell and heaven once given to a pilgrim. First he was given a glimpse of hell, and what he saw was people sitting at a long festive table which was laden with every kind of exotic food and delicacies. The catch was that they had to eat the food with knives and forks which were five feet long. They were yelling their anger and frustration as the food lay temptingly before them and not one morsel could they put to their lips.

Then the pilgrim was taken to heaven and what he saw there was basically the same. The food was exactly similar, the knives and forks were the same length as below, but all were enjoying themselves. Those on one side of the table were using their knives and forks to feed the people on the other side and vice versa. The idea came to them straight away because they had been used to coming to the assistance of others whilst on earth.

17. Wonderful to Be Wanted

...the main plot of existence is not about our
searching for him but about his searching for us.
Buddhism and Hinduism, for instance, are rich
traditions embodying this long quest for spiritual
wisdom. But Christianity is something else because at
its core is a quite different quest: the coming of God
into humanity to seek us out. That search takes the
form of a love story.   *Michael Paul Gallagher*

Francis MacManus tells the story of the Irish poet Donn-
chadh Ruadh Mac Conmara in three novels: *Stand and
Give Challenge, Candle for the Proud,* and *Men Withering*. It
is not unusual to find authors using this form of artistry in
which the same scenes, characters and story feature in three
successive works.

Jesus gave us such a trilogy on just one occasion. It is to be
found in chapter 15 of St. Luke's gospel, where three stories
all form panels of the same picture: The shepherd who lost a
sheep, the woman who lost a coin, and the father who lost a
son. The basic message of this triune parable is that the Son
of Man is come to seek and to save that which is lost.

The trilogy presents a fascinating study of values. It is bad
to lose a sheep, worse to lose money but—witness the land,
sea, and air searches that go on when a man is lost—it is worst
of all to lose a human being.

Then again the sheep is lost and probably knows it is lost,
the coin is lost and has no idea it is lost, but the prodigal is
knowingly and willfully lost. So it is with ourselves; we can
be lost like the sheep, the coin, or the prodigal. However we
are lost, in God's eyes we are well worth saving. There is an

interesting study in attitudes. The sheep wanders on but is overtaken; the coin remains stationary but is found; the prodigal and his father actually move toward one another.

An old lady was asked what was her most cherished memory in life. She thought for a while and then replied, "The day I became engaged." When asked why, she said, "I suppose it was the feeling that somebody wanted me. It is wonderful to be wanted."

H ere is a lovely parable with a similar message by E. V. Lucas:

A mother lost her soldier son. The news came to her in dispatches from the war. He had fallen fighting nobly at the head of his regiment. She was inconsolable.

"Oh that I might see him again," she prayed, "if only for five minutes—but to see him."

An angel answered her prayer. "For five minutes," said the angel, "you will see him, but remember, he was a grown man. There are thirty years to choose from. How would you like to see him?" And the mother paused and wondered.

"Would you see him," said the angel, "as a soldier dying heroically at his post? Would you see him again as on that day at school when he stepped to the platform to receive the highest honor a boy could have?" The mother's eyes lit up. "Would you see him," said the angel, "as a babe at your breast?"

And slowly the mother said, "No, I would have him for five minutes as he was one day when he ran in from the garden to ask my forgiveness for being naughty. He was so small, and so unhappy, and he flew into my arms with such force that he hurt me."

The one thing that the mother wished above all to recapture was the moment when her son needed her. She too could say, "It is wonderful to be wanted."

How true! Happy sheep to be wanted by such a shepherd; happy coin to be wanted by such a searcher; happy son to be wanted by such a father—and happy each one of us when we too realize how much we are wanted.

18. Christmas Stories

A young woman who is pregnant will have a son and
will name him "Immanuel."   *Isaiah 7:14*

Ｏne Christmas day a father was helping his children to
build a snowman. A plane was passing overhead and the
smallest child gazing at it said, "Daddy how do people climb
up into the sky to get into planes?"

"They don't, child," replied the father. "The planes come
down out of the sky to collect the people."

This little anecdote captures the message of Christmas. We
don't have to go up into the sky to find God; he came down
on earth to find us.

Ｏn Christmas morning a very distraught mother came to a
priest friend of mine and told him that her child, a little
boy of six, was missing. He sat her down and listened to her
story.

The child had been writing to Santa for, of all things, a
wheelbarrow, which duly arrived with the Christmas gifts that
morning; needless to say he was up in the moon with
excitement. He disappeared with the wheelbarrow while his
mother was preparing the dinner and his absence went
unnoticed for a couple of hours. The priest decided to go with
her to the police but as the church was just across the road he
suggested that both of them make a brief visit to pray for his

recovery. As they prayed together in the silence of the empty church they heard a noise in the side aisle, and to their astonishment who did they see but the missing child coming toward them, pushing his wheelbarrow! He was not alone, for perched in the wheelbarrow, sitting comfortably on a lump of straw, was the infant from the crib.

Then the story unfolded. It appears that once when he was kneeling with his mother before the crib he entered into a secret pact with the Baby Jesus that if he would use his influence with Santa to get him the wheelbarrow he would take him for a ride in it. True to his promise he climbed into the crib, removed the infant, took some straw to make him comfortable, set him up in the wheelbarrow and spent the best part of two hours wheeling him around the church!

This true incident is a perfect illustration of the fact that Christmas is for children in more senses than presents from Santa Claus. More than the rest of humankind, their faith helps them to grasp the reality of the Christ-child.

Frank O'Connor in his autobiography *An Only Child* tells of a somewhat similar experience.

"One Christmas, Santa Claus brought me a toy engine. I took it with me to the convent and played with it while mother and the nuns discussed old times. A young nun brought us in to see the crib. When I saw the Holy Child in the manger, I was distressed because little as I had, he had nothing at all. For me it was fresh proof of the incompetence of Santa Claus. I asked the young nun politely if the Holy Child didn't like toys, and she replied composedly enough, 'Oh, he does but his mother was too poor to afford them.' That settled it. My mother was poor too, but at Christmas she at least managed to buy me something even if it was only a box of crayons. I distinctly remember getting into the crib and putting the engine between his out-stretched arms. I probably showed him how to wind it as well, because a small baby like that would not be clever enough to know. I remember too the tearful feeling of reckless generosity with which I left him there in the nightly darkness of the chapel, clutching my toy engine to his chest."

There are few religious symbols which catch the imagination of children like the crib. Parents are constantly bringing their children to the crib to tell them the story of Christmas. Many homes have their own little cribs taking pride of place among the Christmas decorations.

According to an adaptation of one of C. H. Spurgeon's stories, in one such home a very good Christian father gathered his family around the crib on the night of Christmas eve. He proposed that the birth of Christ be the subject of their conversation and that every one of the children would say something about it. He would comment on each of their remarks. He called in Mary, the family servant, and when all were seated comfortably he read for them the story of Christ's birth as told by St. Luke.

Then to the youngest boy he said, "What have you to say, Willie?"

Willie remembered a hymn he learned in first grade, and he sung it out:

> Jesus Christ my Lord and Savior
> Once became a child like me.

"Good boy, Willie," responded his father. "Jesus was born into the world as other little babies are born. He was small, delicate, weak, and needed nursing and care. He used to eat, drink, sleep, walk, laugh, and cry like other children."

Then it was John's turn. John was a few years older.

"Well, Dad, if Jesus was like us in some things, he had to do without a lot of the things we have—fire, television, snug bed. It seems to be shocking that he had to live in a stable."

His dad replied, "It makes us think how our blessed Lord cast in his lot with the poor. The wise men when they found him must have been surprised that he was a poor man's child. He was born in another man's stable; he would be buried in another man's grave. Your turn now, Ann."

Ann was at an awkward age. She was a good kid, but not above getting reprimands. She hung her head. "O Daddy, how good Jesus Christ was. He never did anything wrong."

"Very true, he was without fault, without sin and never disappointed any hopes that were set on him."

"There now," continued the father, "we have three beautiful thoughts already: Jesus Christ took our nature, he condescended to be very poor and he was without sin." He turned to the big lad home from college, "You, Dick."

Dick's comment was typically brief. "That child had a wonderful mind."

"Indeed he had. He would say: I am the Way and the Truth and the Life. His was a mind free from evil thoughts, grudges, resentments."

Then he turned to Mary, the servant. "Don't be shy, Mary. Speak out!"

"I was just thinking, Sir," she said, "how humble it was of him to take the form of a servant."

"Yes, Mary," he replied, "he was born in servants' quarters and later he would say, 'I came not to be served but to serve....'"

The mother was taking a quiet interest in all that was shared, then she spoke as a mother.

"What a lovely child! In a few short years he will be overwhelmed with anxiety, suffering and anguish; these hands will be pierced, his face spat upon and Mary his mother will cradle in her arms the lifeless body of the son she bore." There was a pensive sadness on every face as she spoke.

"You have spoken best of all," said her husband, "but remember this is Christmas and what I see is two hands raised in blessing, two hands offering us the Bread of Life, two feet going about doing good, two lips from which would flow streams of eloquence, wisdom and guidance. But the great thing is, he is risen, he is alive, he has conquered death and made hope possible. He has shown us that life does not end with the grave. He is with us and in us."

So ended the series of observations around the Christmas crib. "Time to go to bed," said the father. "Early Mass in the morning. Good night, God bless and a happy Christmas to all."

Night had fallen and the only light was from the flickering flames of a pile of burning stocks. They lit up the faces of the Zulu menfolk sitting round the fire on their mats and sent their shadows dancing on the low, beehive-shaped huts that encircled them.

There were young men there, just returned to the homestead. They had tales to tell of strangers in the land.

"Not like the ones who came before with weapons that spat fire and screeching pebbles. These strangers pay respect to their chiefs, they have comforting words for the sufferer, and they care for the sick.

"And all the time they speak about a wonderful one they call the savior of all men.

"Born in a stable, he was. Important though, because kings came looking for him with gifts of gold. They spoke with power, like our old men reciting the tribal history."

Old Shaka, named after a famous chief, had been taking it all in.

The party dispersed. He crouched down through the low entrance into his hut, spread his mat on the foot of the tree trunk which was the centerpost of the hut, lay down and lowered the back of his head on the wooden headrest. Shaka slipped into sleep and the talk of the evening molded his dreams.

"Gold," he mused in his dream, "I have no gold. But my staff is precious, with its knob carved like the head of a Zulu chief. And powerful. It could beat down many an enemy."

To the child in the stable he offered his staff.

The child said: "All power is given me in heaven and on earth. I come not to strike men down but to love and redeem them. You are kind, Shaka, but keep your staff."

His next most precious possession was a blanket. Off he went to offer that.

But the child said: "Birds have their nests, but the Son of Man will have no place to rest, no comfort." Smiling, he gave back the blanket.

Shaka had no other treasures. "I know what," he said. In his dream he put on his warrior's feathered head-dress and took his shield. "When there is war," he said, "I serve my chief. I will be your warrior in war."

But the child said: "My kingdom is not of this world. If it were, my Father would give me an army of a thousand angels."

Shaka woke up. He took his staff and walked into the dawn.

It was deep in the night when he came at last to a big hut of a place with lights glowing inside. It was full of people, his tribespeople. A tin hurricane lamp hung from a beam.

Leaning on his staff, his fingers twined round the Zulu chief knob, Shaka understood little at that Christmas midnight Mass.

The long catechumenate made everything clear, and at baptism Shaka was named Noel. "Comes from Emmanuel," the missionary explained, "which means, God with us."

And Shaka understood. The child was the Prince of Peace and the kingdom was within.

19. The Road to Holycross

They two then explained to them what had happened
on the road, and how they had recognized the Lord
when he broke the bread.   *Luke 24:35*

Every September people come in the thousands to Holy-cross Abbey for the solemn novena. In the vast congregation on the final Sunday evening was Mary. She told a story that many parents can relate to. For years she had prayed that her two sons would return to the faith. They were uppermost in her thoughts and prayers on this last evening of the festival of faith. Then she looked up and couldn't believe her eyes. Her two sons were standing inside the door of the abbey. Better still, she saw them in a line for confession afterward. Her joy and gratitude overflowed. Afterwards she asked the boys what prompted their return to the faith. The elder son told the story.

That Sunday evening they had been on their way to a dance club. It was raining cats and dogs. Suddenly they came on an old man without an umbrella. He was soaked through and through, and he walked with a noticeable limp. Yet he kept trudging along the road and the brothers stopped to pick him up. It turned out that the stranger was on his way to the novena in Holycross, three miles down the road. The brothers took him there and as it was still raining heavily they decided to wait for him and take him home afterward. It wasn't long before they decided that they might as well go inside. It was better than waiting in the car. Something in the sermon moved them deeply and as they stood during the breaking of bread they made their decision.

19. The Road to Holycross

The story of two brothers and their meeting with the stranger on the road to Holycross bears a striking resemblance to a famous encounter on another road leading to another village at another time.

The two men traveling on the Emmaus road had once been followers of Jesus, and then the terrible events of Good Friday shattered their hopes and dreams. It was against this background that they met the stranger on the road to Emmaus. They listened to him, watched him break bread, and something moved them deeply. The stranger was not a stranger at all. It was Jesus, alive and risen.

Almost the identical thing happened to the two brothers on the road to Holycross. There were the days of childhood, a time of implicit faith and trust in the Lord. Then came the unsettling days of adolescence. Totally disillusioned they no longer followed him but went their own way. It was against this background that they met the stranger one rainy Sunday evening on a Tipperary country road. He spoke to the brothers about Jesus not in words but example, and later in the abbey during the breaking of the bread they discovered the Jesus they had lost.

The story of the disciples on the Emmaus road and the brothers on the road to Holycross is not unlike our own story. As we journey on the road through life there are times when our faith seems to fail and our hopes are shattered, and then we meet some stranger who touches our lives and we find the risen Lord again in the midst of his church, in the breaking of bread.

20. Prayer—The Breakthrough to God

It is seldom one hears priests talking about prayer.
Cardinal Basil Hume, Searching for God

Readers of the influential magazine *U.S. Catholic* were asked to list the topics that they would most like to hear in the Sunday sermon. The one that topped all the others was prayer. Deep down in each one of us there is a desire to know more about prayer; to enter into a personal relationship with God; to experience the power and presence of the Lord in our lives. Christ's words at the Last Supper—"For a long time I have been with you all; yet you do not know me, Philip?" (Jn 14:9)—are illustrated in the following scene from Eugene Ionesco's play, *The Bald Soprano.* Two people who do not know each other are sitting in a room. Their conversation reveals a series of striking coincidences. Both were born in Manchester; each has a two-year-old daughter named Alice; they are now living in London and are actually dwelling on the same street. They live in the same apartment building and share the very same flat. It transpires that they are husband and wife and that they do not know each other.

Isn't this the story of our lives? We live under the same roof as the Lord, we carry his indwelling Spirit about with us, we receive him in the Eucharist and yet we do not know him as a person. We find it difficult to break through to him in prayer, and as a consequence we find it hard to talk about prayer.

In a radical reappraisal of the preaching ministry, David Watson puts his finger on the kernel of the problem. "A man cannot preach Christ unless he knows Christ; he cannot witness to the power of the Holy Spirit unless he knows that power in his own heart; he cannot talk about prayer unless he knows the reality of personal communion with God. Spiritual truths must become a part of a man before they can be effectively preached by that man."

In the light of these words my own conscience is beginning to bother me so I'm going to seek refuge in a story! This one illustrates some of the situations in which we can seek the Lord's face in prayer.

An American football coach has written a book called *I Believe*. It is based on a harrowing experience shared by himself and his team.

They were returning by chartered flight from an away game when the plane developed serious trouble and the captain announced that he had no choice but to attempt a crash landing. He couldn't jettison fuel so an explosion was likely. As the plane sped downward one of the players cried out, "Coach, lead us in prayer!" The coach got to his feet and prayed for deliverance for everybody. Then the plane hit the ground and plowed through a field before finally coming to a halt. No one was injured. Next day the coach was in the church with his family. He thanked the Lord for his protection and deliverance. After service he sent his family home and he by himself went down to the team's clubrooms. In the dressing room where he used give his team pep talks he knelt down and prayed: "Lord, I know that you have a plan, a purpose and a will for my life and the lives of these young men. I do not know what it is but I'll try to impress upon the young men I coach this year and forever that there is more to life than just playing football—that you have a purpose for our lives."

Notice how this pattern of prayer so closely resembles that of Christ. The coach prayed alone in the dressing room, he prayed in the small group situation on the plane, and he prayed as part of the wider community at church on Sunday.

The Scriptures record numerous instances where the Lord prayed in similar situations. He was constantly slipping off to pray on his own in lonely places. On one occasion he spent a whole night in prayer on a hillside. He prayed in the group situation with his apostles, particularly Peter, James and John, and he went to the synagogue to pray every Sabbath "as was his custom."

There is a useful pattern of prayer here for us too. There are times when we need to be alone with God, times when we need the strength and support of the group as in family prayer or prayer meetings, and times such as on Sundays when we come together to pray as members of a worshiping community. The following incident is an example of prayer in the group situation.

A British army unit was recently patrolling the border town of Warrenpoint. The soldiers were surprised to hear singing from a pub that had been recently devastated by a bomb. Entering, they found over sixty people with hymn-books assembled in the burnt-out bar. When the startled officer asked if the bar was open he was told, "We're open for prayer. Why not join us?"

What the army patrol stumbled on could provide a ray of hope in the agony of Northern Ireland. It was one of the many prayer groups dedicated to forgiveness and reconciliation, which today represent one of the fastest growing movements in Christianity. These people claim to have rediscovered the Holy Spirit and through charismatic renewal, as it is popularly called, people have returned to believe in "the Lord, the giver of life," as the Nicene Creed names the Spirit.

A priest once noticed a member of his Sunday congregation who seemed to be rapt in prayer all through the Mass. Eager to learn from her experience he asked her on one occasion how she spent the time and what form her prayer took.

"I say the Our Father," was her simple response.

"But surely you do more than that," he countered.

"No," she said, "you see when I'm in good form for praying all I say is the first two words: Our Father. When I'm only in middling form I'm able to get half-way through it but if there's something on my mind and I'm in real bad form, I can finish it and maybe say it two or three times." Here was contemplative prayer at its best.

People in prayer are sermons in themselves. Take the case of Mary Ryan. For twenty-five years she lay suffering from cancer in a hospital bed and in all that time not one word of complaint ever passed her lips. It was my privilege to minister to her for the best part of twenty years and the abiding memory will always be the ever-present smiles, serenity in the face of pain, and lips constantly moving in prayer. When I'd greet her, "How are you today, Mary?" the reply was predictable, "Grand, Father, thanks be to God and his blessed Mother." I always came away enriched, feeling that I was the one who was the beneficiary of the visit.

Once in a radio Mass from the Hospital of the Assumption in Thurles where she was a patient I told her story in the course of the homily. It was the Feast of All Saints and I suggested that the saints whom we were honoring on this day were the Mary Ryans of this world. Two days later I received a letter from a doctor. "For the past twelve months," he wrote, "I have been confined to bed as a result of a serious car accident. I was a keen sportsman with a very successful medical practice. I could not accept what happened to me and in my bitterness I lost faith in God and man. As I lay in bed in the depth of depression on Sunday morning I switched on the radio and heard you tell the story of Mary Ryan and her heroic acceptance of a cross far greater than mine. Please thank her from me for restoring a lost faith."

Another story centers on one of the shortest prayers ever said—just three words: "Jesus 'tis Jim."

A priest was deeply concerned over the frequent visits of a poorly clad stranger to his church. What aroused his suspicions was the nature of the visits. The man would come in, stand for a few seconds at the back of the church and then leave. Concerned for his shrine boxes the priest told the sacristan to keep a close eye on him. One day the sacristan accosted him and asked him what he was doing. "Just talking to the Lord," was the reply.

"How could you?" said the other. "You're no sooner in than you're out again. Do you call that prayer?"

Then the stranger replied, "I just look up at him and I say 'Jesus, 'tis Jim.'"

Some time afterward the priest was visiting one of the wards in the hospital and a nurse told him of a newcomer to the ward and the amazing effect he had on the other patients. No one seemed to know where he was from, no one ever came to see him, but there was something special about him. There was no longer any bad language or dirty jokes, the angelus and rosary were said with extra fervor, and all in all the man seemed to radiate goodness.

When the priest went to his bedside he instantly recognized him as the church visitor whom he had rashly misjudged. Anxious to learn he asked him about his prayer life, his joyful serenity, and the influence he was exercising on the other patients.

"It's my visitor, Father," came the reply. Knowing that the man had no visitors the priest was about to interject when the man continued, "Yes, Father, he comes to me every day and stands there at the food of the bed. He looks and me and he says, 'Jim—it's Jesus!'"

Once I sat by the death-bed of a priest and as I watched him die I asked if there was anything I could do for him. The reply startled me. "Pray with me," he said, "because I can't think and I can't pray." Apart from the fact that I didn't have *The Pastoral Care of the Sick* with me at the time, my usual crutch in these situations, I felt a real sense of inadequacy in this instance, because here I was dealing with a man of God whose ministry had been a living prayer in itself. I thought to myself then and many times since: My God, if he can't pray as he leaves this world, what hope for me! Our priesthood is never more challenged than in the pastoral care of the dying. If we can't pray with them and give them a sense of Christ at this time, our role becomes purely functional. We dole out the sacraments and rely on the old *ex opere operato* to do the rest.

Once as a priest was leaving the bedside of a dying man he pointed to the chair he had just vacated and said, "Every time you look at that empty chair try to see Christ sitting in it. You just look at him and prayer will come easy."

The advice worked and the story goes that shortly afterward the man's daughter called on the priest to tell him that her father had died. She said, "I spent his last hours with him. He just seemed to radiate peace and serenity. Then I left the room for about twenty minutes. When I returned he was dead and the strange thing is, his head was resting not on the pillows but on a chair that was beside his bed."

21. Now...I'll Call upon Father...

Every man who is happily married is a successful man even if he has failed in everything else.

William Lyon Phelps

There's a plethora of wedding stories, most of them as predictable and as vulgar as the telegrams that have to be endured at the reception. The priest is expected to interlace his speech with stories and he invariably extols the virtues of his side of the partnership. You know what I mean. "We're sorry to be losing Bridget....She comes from a fine decent upstanding family....I've known Bill and Kate Murphy for a long time...." And so on and so forth! On one occasion the parish priest went overboard in his praise of the Ryans. He traced their lineage back to the flood and how Noah, fearing that such an illustrious family might be lost like the unicorn, took two of them on the Ark—which accounts for the proliferation of Ryans today!

The other side, not to be outdone, claimed their pedigree went back just as far only, unlike the Ryans, the Murphys didn't have to go on the Ark—they had their own boat!

A feature of weddings in more recent times is the lighting of the candles. The couple light two before the ceremony, signifying their individual lives, then when they become husband and wife they blow them out and light a single candle to symbolize the two becoming one and the unity of the partnership henceforth.

On one occasion when not only the candles but also the readings proclaimed their unity, the couple were walking down the aisle after signing the register, and as they beamed at the admiring guests the bride gave her newly acquired husband a nudge and whispered, "Did you take all that in?"

"All what?" he said.

"All that about the two being one."

"Yes, I guess so," he said, and then came the *coup de grace*.

"Well, in case you're in any doubt, from now on *I'm the one!*"

Then there was the occasion when some forty or so of the men of the parish went to Limerick on a weekend retreat. One of the lecturers had just returned from a stint in the States and he had some harsh things to say to them about their love lives. He contended that the Irish male remained a bachelor at heart after his marriage, evidenced by the fact that he never remembered anniversaries, scarcely ever took his wife out, and was still one of the boys in the pub. Compared with his American counterpart he was "a lousy lover."

He told them how the American was much more demonstrative in his affection for his wife, how he kissed her before leaving for work in the morning and first thing when he came home in the evening, how thoughtful he was in remembering birthdays, wedding anniversaries and special occasions like Mother's Day, and how he wouldn't dream of going out in the evening without her. All things considered, by comparison the Irish husband was a sorry specimen!

At least one of his listeners took these words to heart and was filled with remorse by what he heard. Alone in his austere monastery bedroom, he reflected ruefully on the comforts of home and on the tender loving care lavished on him by his much taken-for-granted wife. All this sinful neglect got to him so much that he just couldn't wait to get home to make amends.

When the retreat ended on Sunday evening there was one last fling with the boys after which he returned home to find his ever-loving wife in bed and asleep. So he decided to defer repentance and reparation until the following evening. In the aftermath of subsequent events he admitted to me that he "might have overdone it." At any rate he arrived home from work next day armed with a beautiful bouquet, made straight for the kitchen where Mary was preparing the evening meal, pushed the flowers on her and then threw his arms around her and kissed her.

Imagine his astonishment when the wife immediately burst into tears. "What's wrong?" he gasped.

"Everything's wrong," she cried. "I've had a migraine all day. Tommy had a fall at school so I had to take him to the doctor and have him stitched. On the way home I had a flat tire and I got back here to find the electricity cut off! My God what a day," she bawled, "and now you crown it all by coming home drunk!"

This collection has been regularly punctuated by intrusions from Lena, my housekeeper, asking, "How's the book?" The most recent one came while I was writing this section and it called to mind a romantic interlude in her life which would tend to confirm the views of that priest in Limerick.

It appears that on one occasion she was extremely flattered by a proposal of marriage from a farmer whom she had just met.

"I'm not the marrying type," said she, "and besides, I'm not so sure I'd make a good wife."

"Don't mind the wife bit," came the not-so-romantic reply. "To tell you the truth, 'tis for round the yard I want you!"

I narrated this incident to a classmate, now a parish priest in Clare, and he didn't seem all that surprised. "There's a few of these fellows around yet," he declared, adding, "I've one of them in my parish. We're trying to marry him off for years but the devil wouldn't please him. I said to him once: 'Mick, what in God's name are you looking for in a wife.'"

"'I'll tell you, Father,' came the reply, 'what I'm looking for is one that'll be between two buckets in the cowshed at seven o'clock in the morning!'"

Here is a Hindu fable on the creation of woman, which contains pertinent and possibly useful advice:

God took the roundness of the moon and the litheness of the serpent, the clinging of the creeper and the trembling of the grass, the soft glance of the deer and the fickleness of the wind, the weeping of the rain-cloud and the gayness of the sunshine, the shyness of the hare and the vanity of the peacock, the sugary sweetness of honey and the cruelty of the tiger, the coldness of snow and the warmth of fire, the chatter of the jay and the cooing of the dove....All these things he mingled together and out of them he made Woman.

She was gracious and alluring, and, finding her more beautiful than the ibis or the gazelle, God admired her exceedingly and was proud of his work, so he made a present of her to man.

A week later man came to God in distress:

"Look, Lord, the creature whom you have given me is the plague of my life. She talks incessantly and is ever complaining about nothing; she laughs and cries together; she is restless, exacting and fidgety; she is always running after me; she never gives me a moment's rest. Please, Lord, take her back again, for I cannot live with her."

And God, like a good father, took her back again. But a week later man came to God again: "Lord, I am very lonely since you have taken that creature away from me. She used to sing and dance before me; and how entrancing was her glance when she looked at me out of the corner of her eyes, without turning her head! She used to play with me, and no fruit upon the trees is so sweet as were her caresses. Please give her back to me, for I cannot live without her." And God gave woman back to him.

Another week passed, and God frowned as he saw man approaching him again, pushing the woman before him. "Lord," he said, "I know not how it is, but I am certain that this creature gives me more annoyance than pleasure. Please take her back again."

Hearing these words, God was angry! "Man, go back to your hut with your companion, and try to put up with her. If I kept her you would only come back again in a week, imploring me to give her to you again!" And man went away.

"Unhappy creature that I am," he said. "With her I cannot live, and I cannot live without her!"

There is one lovely story which is equally suited to the wedding homily and "Father's few words" at the reception. It is a story of caring, unselfish love. A young couple who had just been married were driving off on their honeymoon. It was night and they were on a lonely stretch of road when they were suddenly engulfed in a violent thunderstorm. They drove with difficulty through the blinding rain until they saw the lights of an isolated farmstead. They abandoned their car and ran to the house. The door was opened by an elderly couple who welcomed them. They explained their plight and asked if they could stop over for the night, saying that they were quite prepared to sleep on the kitchen chairs. The old woman noticed the rice in the bride's hair and looking knowingly at the husband said they'd give the young couple the visitor's room. "I'll just go and freshen it up," she said. The following morning when the newlyweds awoke the sun was shining, and deciding to leave early they left ten pounds on the dressing table and crept silently downstairs so as not to disturb their hosts. As they entered the living room they saw the old man and his wife asleep on the two chairs. Then it dawned on them that the old pair had given them their one and only bedroom. The young man whispered to his wife to wait as he climbed the stairs again and placed another tenner on the dressing table.

22. The End of Life's Story

The last act is always a tragedy, whatever fine comedy there may have been in the rest of life. We must all die alone.   *Blaise Pascal*

The life of each of us is a story, and a unique story at that. It is a tale of joys and sorrows, of hopes and disappointments, of successes and failures, of pleasure and pain. The story of my life ends with death, or does it? Every death is unique; every sense of loss is unique; every expression of grief is unique because everyone's story is unique.

The whole area of death and bereavement presents the priest with possibly his greatest pastoral challenge. In his ministry to the dying he is in a sense writing the last chapter in the story of a life and in so doing he creates cherished memories which will be recalled and remembered when the story is re-told. In helping people to cope with grief and bereavement he needs to be a good listener and a person of great compassion and sensitivity. Because each parting is unique his homily should bring a special message of comfort and hope. Illustrations in the funeral homily are hardly necessary because the casket before the altar and the grief in the front pews are the most compelling of all illustrations. Funeral homilies are a special challenge to the preacher. Everyone has a story to tell, especially in time of bereavement. Whenever we go to a home to express our sympathy we invariably listen to people in their grief telling stories about the loved one they lost. If the preacher is a caring listener he should have no difficulty with his funeral homily the following day. He will re-tell the family's stories in the context of the Lord's comforting story of hope and resurrection.

22. The End of Life's Story

Despite the fact that the media are daily bombarding us with stories of death and disaster, the people of God do not like to hear sermons on death. It is all part of the modern outlook, which tends to downplay the reality of death or to think of it in terms of the other person. We can all be philosophical when speaking of other people's troubles, but it's only when death touches our own lives in the loss of a loved one that we tend to look at ourselves *sub specie aeternitatis*. The certainty of death, the uncertainty of the time, place, and circumstances, and the Christian messages of hope and life after death need to be affirmed in our preaching from time to time. The following illustrations may be of some assistance.

A young man was in the market-place in Baghdad when he saw a woman casting threatening glances at him. He recognized her instantly as Death, and terrified he ran to his master, begging him for a horse so that he could flee from the city. When asked the reason for his sudden departure he said, "I've just seen Death in the market-place and she was threatening me. Please, please give me a horse so that I can get away to Somara." The master gave him the horse, wished him God speed, and the young man galloped like a madman to Somara which was twenty miles away. Then his master went down to the market-place where he too saw Death. He went up to her and asked why she was threatening his servant.

"I wasn't threatening him," Death replied. "I was surprised to see him in Baghdad, because tonight I have an appointment with him in Somara."

A sixteen-year-old girl lay dying in the hospital. A priest went to visit her and as he sat by her bedside his face showed obvious distress. Then to his amazement the girl put her hand on his and said, "Do not be afraid, Father. Do not be afraid." Here in the face of death the child was comforting the adult, the girl reassuring the priest, the dying consoling the living.

This true incident recalls the last moments of the saintly English king, Edward the Confessor. Seeing his friends and relatives grieving by his bedside he said to them. "Do not cry. I leave the land of the dying to go to the land of the living."

Sometimes God sends his love letters in black-edged envelopes," said Spurgeon. "He allows us to taste the bitterness of want and the desolation of bereavement. If you have lived many years, you have passed the narrows. We have all been there. It looks as if things have got out of hand, and somehow or other we have been forgotten. When there is no one at hand to say it to you, say to yourself, 'God is faithful…who will not suffer the pain to exceed the measurement of my endurance'" (1 Cor 10:13; [see also] Heb 12:6,11).

The great Methodist preacher William E. Sangster has a fine story on how values change in the face of death.

"It was just after ten o'clock on the night of 14 April 1912 that the *Titanic,* the largest vessel then afloat, crashed in mid-Atlantic into an iceberg and four hours later went to the bottom. Much has been written of all that took place in those four hours. Survivors spoke of the calm heroism of the captain, the officers, and the crew. They told also of the courage of the bandmaster who played 'Nearer, My God, to Thee' while he struggled into his life belt, and they said that many women, who could have been rescued, refused the offer, preferring to drown with their husbands.

"They told another story also, less courageous but more curious than any of these.

"A certain woman, who had been allotted a place in one of the boats, asked if she might run back to her state-room, and she was given three minutes to go. She hurried along the corridors already tilting at a dangerous angle, and crossed the saloon. Money and costly gems littered the floor. Some who snatched at their jewelry spilt it as they ran. In her own state-room she saw her treasure waiting to be picked up. She saw—and took no heed. Snatching at three oranges which she knew to be there, she took her place in the boat.

"That little incident is instructive. An hour before, it would have seemed incredible to that woman that she could have preferred a few oranges to one small diamond, but Death boarded the *Titanic* and, with one blast of his awful breath, all values were transformed. Precious things became worthless; worthless things became precious. Oranges were more precious than diamonds."

Once the court jester was summoned to brighten the last hours of a dying king with his wit and humor. But all his best jokes and witticisms could not even evoke a smile from the monarch. "Why are you so sad, Sire?" said the jester.

"Because I am about to leave on a journey," was the reply.

"Is the journey a long one?"

"It is the longest journey I've ever made," said the king.

The jester looked around the room and then asked, "But if you're going on such a long journey how come you're not prepared? I see no suitcase, no clothes, no horses."

"Ah, that's the problem," replied the king. "I've been so preoccupied with other things that I didn't find time to prepare for the journey and now I've got to face it alone."

"Here," said the jester, taking off his cap and bells, "you take these because I see now that you're an even bigger fool than I am. You're going on a long journey unprepared and all you can do is bring me here to amuse you!"

This is a good story and a telling one to convince people that there is a journey of supreme importance facing all of us when this little life is over.

Timothy lay dying and his ever-loving Mary Kate was in the kitchen, trying to cope with her grief as she mixed the ingredients of her husband's favorite fruit cake. She tearfully placed the cake in the oven and soon the aroma wafted its way to the nostrils of the dying man.

"Mary Kate," he called feebly.

"Yes, darling," she replied tenderly as she came running to his beside. "What is it, dear?"

"Could I have a tiny piece of that cake for old times' sake?"

"No way," said Mary Kate as she flounced back to her kitchen. "I'm keeping that for your wake!"

Have you ever noticed the spate of eulogies that come in the wake of a loved one's passing? Memories are recreated, nice things are said, and of course there are the inevitable regrets that these nice things weren't said while the person was living. The word "eulogy," which means "a good word," is now exclusively identified with death because seldom or ever do we praise the living. So often we grieve over the if-onlys and the might-have-beens. "If only I had told her how much I loved her.... I could have been nicer to him!" Why not start now? Kind words come cheaply but they can mean a lot in the final chapter of someone's story. In other words, do not save the cake for the wake!

Until I became a priest I had never seen anyone die. Shortly after ordination I went to a saintly old priest, seeking advice on the pastoral care of the dying. He told me that the first person he had anointed and seen into eternity was his parish priest. He was over-awed by the occasion as the pastor was one of those truly great missionary priests who left Ireland before the end of the last century to blaze a trail for Christ in the Antipodes. He was a legend in his lifetime, who created flourishing Christian communities in every area where he ministered. His one pastime was to walk the hills with his dog and gun. Noticing how nervous his assistant was in administering the last rites he said to him by way of reassurance, "John, will you do one thing for me?"

And willing to do anything to comfort the dying man, he replied, "Sure, Father, anything you ask."

"John," said he with a twinkle in his eye, "would you ever put the gun into the coffin with me. I might get a shot when I'm passing through the Valley of Jehosaphat!"

Probably the clearest vision of life after death was the one given by God to John, the Seer of Patmos, on a rocky island in the eastern Mediterranean where the Romans had exiled him.

His book, Revelation, the last one in the Bible, is all about judgment and the victory of God. It has been likened to a tunnel with light at the beginning (chapters 1-5) and in the middle a long stretch of darkness full of dragons, monsters, plagues and catastrophes, but when we grope our way to the end of the tunnel the world of the past is gone and we are in the light again, this time perpetual light, a light that never ends.

This vision is so symbolic of our own lives, reborn as we are into the light at baptism, then that brief period of childhood innocence and trusting faith before entering the tunnel of doubt, despair, suffering, and all the other "ills that flesh is heir to." Sustained by a higher hope we finally emerge to the vision of the New Jerusalem where "God," says the heavenly voice, "will wipe away all tears from their eyes. There will be no more death, no more grief or crying or pain, the old things have disappeared" (Rev 21:4).

23. Long Memories and Forgiveness

An unwillingness to forgive others for the real or
imaginary wrongs they have done is a poison that
affects our health—physical, emotional and
spiritual—sometimes very deeply. You commonly hear
people say, "I can forgive, but I cannot forget" or "I
want to forgive but cannot." What they really mean is
they do not want to forgive.   *Anthony De Mello*

An aircraft full of American tourists was approaching Belfast. The captain switched on the intercom and made the following announcement, "Ladies and gentlemen, we will shortly be landing at Aldergrove Airport, Belfast. Would you please put your watches back...three hundred years."

Yes, we do have long memories! One of my longest memories is the teacher in primary school impressing on us the need for forgiveness! Children have short memories so forgiveness wasn't really a problem for us.

Of course there are some exceptions, like the two little boys who had an almighty row. At bedtime, the eldest one, Liam, was haranguing his younger brother Seán, and his mother called him aside. "Liam, you shouldn't let the sun go down on your anger."

"I can't stop it, can I?" was the surly reply.

"Look, Liam!" said his mother, "Seán could die tonight and if he did you'd never forgive yourself. You'd always remember that the last thing you did was to fight with him. I know he was rotten to you, but go on now and forgive him before he goes to sleep."

Away went Liam and this is what Mother heard.

"Seán, I've come to forgive you in case you die tonight. But if you don't die tonight, watch out 'cause I'll plaster you in the morning!"

That was forgiveness under compulsion and wasn't much good!

The teacher told us of another quarrel which was much more serious.

There was a deep-rooted running feud between the Kellys and the Murphys. No one seemed to know how it originated but grievances real and imaginary were nurtured and passed on from one generation to another. Old man Kelly was dying and the priest who attended him in his last illness did his utmost to effect a reconciliation between the two families. He pleaded with the old man to forgive the Murphys, but old man Kelly was obdurate. Then he told him that he would shortly face the Lord in judgment and things would go hard with him unless he buried the hatchet.

The fear of judgment apparently mellowed the old man—he reluctantly agreed to forgiveness. Then the priest insisted that he communicate his decision to his five strapping sons, who were called in to the dying man's bedside.

"Well, sons," he said, "I've made my peace with God and I've forgiven the Murphys!" The stunned silence which greeted the declaration of a truce was then shattered by his final words, "But remember this: I'll turn in my grave if one of you forgives them!"

Forgiveness does not come easy. So often we nurse grudges, bitterness and resentments. We bring our gifts to the altar on Sunday and try not to remember the things that our brother has against us.

I can remember as a child being taken on holidays to Dun Laoghaire and seeing a man walking up and down outside a pub in the town. He was wearing sandwich boards which proclaimed, "Strike on here." It turned out to be the longest strike in the history of industrial relations in Ireland. It started in 1939 when publican Pat Downey fired a barman. When he refused to rehire him the pickets began their marathon walk up and down outside the licensed premises. Each year Downey observed the anniversary of the strike by dressing his pub in flags and inviting the pickets in for drinks. If they failed to show up he would ring the union headquarters to know why. When Pat Downey died in 1953, striker Val Murphy put aside his sandwich board and walked into the pub to offer his sympathy to the widow.

Bishop Fulton Sheen used to tell a story of heroic forgiveness. It was narrated to him by a close friend, an Austrian doctor who emigrated with his wife to the United States after the Second World War. Toward the end of the war he was living in eastern Austria with his wife, who was a Jewish convert to Catholicism. The Germans were retreating before the Russians when late one night the doctor was roused from his sleep by a loud banging on the front door. Putting on a dressing-gown he opened the door to a fleeing German officer looking for food and rest. He recognized the SS uniform and when the German gave his name he asked him if he were the Gestapo man responsible for the massacre of the Jews in a certain place. The German affirmed that he was. "Tell me," the doctor continued, "how many Jews did you kill in that place?"

"All of them," was the reply.

The doctor then went into the hall and called to his wife, "Rachel, come down, I want you to meet someone." When his wife entered the room he said to her: "Now, Rachel, I want you to meet the man who killed your father and mother, your grandmother, your sister and two brothers." After the initial shock she went over to the SS officer, put her arms around his neck and said to him, "If God has forgiven you, I too forgive you!"

Erskine Childers was an Englishman with a distinguished war record and the author of *The Riddle of the Sands*. Convinced of the justice for Ireland cause, he was in the forefront of the fight for freedom against the British. He was executed by the Irish Provisional Government on 10 November 1922 for possessing a small revolver given to him by Michael Collins. Before his death he shook hands with each of the firing squad. There was no rancor in his heart as he forgave his executioners.

A few years ago United Airlines flight 629 exploded in the skies above Colorado. Someone had hidden a bomb on the plane and all aboard were killed. Amongst those who died were the parents of three young boys in Pittsburgh. When their parish priest was discussing the funeral service with them one of them asked, "Could we also say a prayer for the man who killed my father and mother?"

Stories like these from real life can be powerful illustrative sermon material. Let us finish with a prayer. It was found near the body of a dead youth in Ravensbruck concentration camp. It reads:

> O Lord, remember
> not only the men and women of goodwill
> but also those of ill-will.
> Do not remember
> all the sufferings they inflicted on us;
> remember the fruits we have borne
> thanks to this suffering—
> our comradeship, our loyalty,
> our humility, our courage
> our generosity, our greatness of heart
> and when they come to judgment
> let all the fruits that we have borne
> be their forgiveness.

24. "Now Listen to *My* Story"

God made man because he loves stories.   *Elie Wiesel*

Even though she failed to supply a title for the book, I am still indebted to my housekeeper for providing the caption for this chapter. It is the recurring prelude to Lena's story, which I listen to daily in what can be described as a captive situation when I'm either at my desk or sampling her culinary delights at the table. The ending is as predictable as the introduction. "That's my story for you, now!" she says, dusting an imaginary speck as she clears away the dishes.

Everyone, like Lena, has a story to tell. The preacher must be a good listener to the people's stories if he is to evoke a response when he proclaims God's story on Sunday. I once heard a preacher speaking on loneliness. It was obvious from his story that he had been through his own Gethsemane, and the stillness in the church showed that he had struck a responsive chord in the listeners. He made the point that everyone's sense of loneliness was unique but that if one were to categorize, then the loneliness of the housewife and mother was probably the most poignant of all. As he spoke the heads of almost three hundred women bowed in unison. Here was a storyteller who was also a story-listener.

"Sure nobody will be listening to you anyway!" These cryptic words, again emanating from Lena on an occasion when I expressed some anxiety about the content of my Sunday homily, had a two-fold message. First, the basic elements of a homily are the preacher, the message, and the listener, so if the listener switches off, the other two fall by the wayside; the preacher labors in vain because the message is lost. Secondly, as we have seen, the amount of time the average Sunday worshiper can listen to a sustained argument is strictly limited. The following story is a case in point.

It was mission-time in a remote rural parish that had been relatively untouched by the upheaval and changes of the Second Vatican Council. Word had got about that the men conducting the mission were of the new way of thinking and that they had disturbed many cherished beliefs and practices with their new-fangled ideas. So the people decided to boycott the mission. On the first night when the preacher came out for the opening sermon he was faced with empty pews. Then he noticed one man sitting by himself toward the rear of the church. The news of the boycott had not reached him since he lived all alone in a mountain cottage. The missioner walked down to him and questioned the merit of preaching to a congregation of one.

"Now look," said the man, "twice a day I go out with the bucket and I feed the hens and if I find that there's only one hen to be fed, well I'll feed her."

The priest got the message and on his way back to the pulpit he decided to give a package deal. He would give the lone attender two sermons instead of one, not to be dragging him down the mountain too often and saving himself time and effort into the bargain. His preaching done he came down to the man again and asked what he thought of the sermon.

"Now look here," came the reply, "didn't I tell you before you started that I'm always prepared to feed only one hen if she comes to me. I didn't say that I'd throw the whole bloomin' bucket at her!"

Another story tells of a rural area devastated by floods resulting in great loss of property and livestock. The village was particularly hard hit and one lady who was marooned in her house watched from her ground floor window as the water lapped her window sill. A boat stopped by and the boatman asked her to come aboard and save herself, but she refused, saying, "I trust in God—he will save me." The boatman shook his head and passed on. The water mounted and as she waited at an upstairs window another boat came by and again she was asked to come aboard. She thanked the boatman and repeated, "I trust in God—he will save me." The man shook his head and rowed on. As the flood waters gradually engulfed the house she went on to the roof where she was spotted by a helicopter. As it hovered over her a ladder was let down and a voice came through a loudspeaker, "Grab the ladder and we'll pull you to safety."

"No," she shouted back, "I trust in God. I am waiting for him to save me." Needless to say she was drowned and when she was admitted to heaven she chided the Lord about how he let her drown and did not come to her help despite all the trust she placed in him.

"But, Lady," replied the Lord, "what more could I have done to help you? Didn't I send you two boats and a helicopter!"

This story illustrates the point that God acts in our lives in the ordinary events and situations in which we find ourselves. We should not be looking for signs or wonders but rather seek him in the ordinary things of life.

Then there's the story of the old monk who had sought to sanctify himself through doing the ordinary things of life extraordinarily well and who felt that now in the latter end of his days he was entitled to a vision from God. He prayed daily for a vision to strengthen his faith and was about to give up hope when one afternoon he entered his cell to find the vision awaiting him. He was just about entering a state of ecstasy when he heard the monastery bell ringing. The poor were at the gate, waiting to be fed, and today it was his turn to serve.

He had to make an agonizing choice: Should he stay on with the vision or go where duty called? Sadly he went to the gates where he fed the poor and then slowly retraced his steps to the monastery. Imagine his joy when he entered his cell to find the vision awaiting him. "If you had not gone to minister to me at the gates," said the vision, "I would not have stayed on here." The message was clear. The monk learned that the best way to serve God was to reach out to him in the poor.

Once a poor family in Eastern Europe were compelled to dig up their roots and emigrate to America. Their friends and neighbors got together and gave them bread and cheese as parting gifts. They were equally poor and could afford to give them little else. They got enough bread and cheese to see them through to the new world.

They traveled steerage in an old steam-ship and confined themselves to their cabin for the entire voyage to preserve their meager savings. All their meals consisted of bread and cheese and this went on for weeks. On the evening before they were due to disembark, the youngest child, a boy of nine, pleaded with his father to let him have just one apple because he was sick of bread and cheese. The father after much persuasion reluctantly gave him a couple of pence to go up on deck and buy an apple. He also gave him strict instructions to return immediately to the cabin.

The boy left and when he hadn't returned after a considerable time the parents became very anxious and his father went up on deck in search of him. He looked into the ship's dining room and to his surprise saw the boy sitting down to a beautiful dinner surrounded by exotic food. Thinking of the expense he rushed in to reprimand him but halted in his tracks when his son exclaimed, "But Daddy, it is all free. We could have had it from the beginning. It was all part of the package, and we settled for bread and cheese!"

As we work our passage through life, how often we settle for bread and cheese without realizing all that is in the package, especially the presence and the power of the Lord's indwelling Spirit!

Flannery O'Connor died in 1964 at the age of thirty-nine. Her passing marked the loss of one of this century's most gifted short story artists. Brought up in an old Catholic family in the bible-belt of the American South she was, in the words of V. S. Pritchett, "saturated in the inner lives of her people." In her first published work, *Wise Blood,* she tells the story of Hazel Motes from the evangelical Deep South, the grandson of a preacher who has "Jesus in him like a sting." At eighteen he is sent to the war and he comes home crippled and disillusioned. Right in the heart of the bible-belt he decides to set up his own anti-church, the Church without Christ. "I'm member and preacher to that church where the blind don't see and the lame don't walk and what's dead stays that way. Ask me about that church and I'll tell you it's the church that the blood of Jesus don't foul with redemption."

"Parker's Back," one of her stories in *Everything that Rises Must Converge,* is a classic example of bible-fed self-righteousness. It tells the story of O. E. Parker, an ignorant truck driver with a passion for having his body tattooed. His wife, Sarah Ruth, belongs to a fundamentalist Protestant sect. She despises his tattoos and is forever berating him for his lack of religiosity. In a desperate effort to regain her affection he takes himself off to the tattooist and presents his back, the only clean canvas left on his body, for the most costly and painful operation yet. He returns to his run-down shack with a large picture of Christ covering his entire back, but Sarah Ruth is not impressed.

"Don't you know who it is?" says Parker. "It's him! It's God!"

Sarah Ruth snarls, "God don't look like that! He's a spirit and no one's ever seen his face."

Parker groans, "Aw, it's just a picture!"

"Idolatry," screams his Sarah Ruth. Then she grabs the poker and begins beating Parker savagely across his back.

Flannery O'Connor concludes her touching story like this: Parker sat there and let her beat him senseless and large welts had formed on the face of the tattooed Christ. Then he staggered up and made for the door.

Later when Sarah Ruth glanced outside her eyes hardened even more. There was Parker leaning against a pecan tree crying like a baby. His tears were not from the savage beating. They were from the fact that Parker now realized there was nothing he could do to please his self-righteous wife.

In a letter written before she died and quoted in her last novel, *The Violent Bear It Away,* Flannery O'Connor explains what she felt about the strange goings-on in the bible-belt: "The religion of the South is a do-it-yourself religion, something which I as a Catholic find painful and touching and grimly comic. It's full of unconscious pride that lands them in all sorts of ridiculous religious predicaments. They have nothing to correct their practical heresies and so they work them out dramatically. If this were merely comic to me, it would be no good, but I accept the same fundamental doctrines of sin and redemption and judgment that they do."

"They work them out dramatically." The caring preacher will find many such situations in the stories of his people if only he takes the time to listen.

25. The Singer and the Song

Late in life I have begun to grasp why some pulpits confront the preacher graphically with the request of the Greeks to Philip: "Sir, we would like to see Jesus" (Jn 12:21). How simple a request...and how stunning! Here is our burden and our joy: to help believing Christians to see Jesus not with our eyes, but with their own.   *Walter S. Burghardt, SJ*

I *have a song to sing, O.* By way of epilogue we return to our tragic jester Jack Point. He rings down the curtain on *Yeoman of the Guard* by telling his story in response to the people's "What is your song, O?"

> It is sung to the moon, by a love-lorn loon
> Who fled from the mocking throng, O!
> It's the song of a merryman moping mum,
> Whose soul was sad, and whose glance was glum,
> Who sipped no sup, and who craved no crumb,
> As he sighed for the love of a lady!

Each of us, preacher and listener, has a song to sing. The preacher's song is the story of God. When the final curtain falls, so much will depend on the singer, his song, and how he listened to the song of his people. The song must make Christ visible through the transparency of the singer's own person. "What you are," said Emerson, "speaks so loudly that I cannot hear what you are saying." As we go through life all of us encounter people whose stories touch our lives in a special way and whose songs make the melody linger on. As my final offering, let me tell you of two rather special people from the early days of my ministry, one a bishop, the other a priest colleague, two men who in telling the story of God told their own story of faith with all its weaknesses and imperfections. They too had their songs to sing, songs which struck a responsive chord in many hearts. What follows is a poor and inadequate rendition of their melody.

Peter McKeefry, Archbishop of Wellington and Primate of New Zealand, was over six feet tall, lean, restless and full of nervous energy. In modern media jargon he was "imposed" on the clergy of Wellington from outside. Naturally they would have preferred one of their own, but from the time he arrived amongst them with two suitcases containing all his worldly possessions, they took him to their hearts. He was a man of touching humility with no interest in the trappings of his office, wearing his cardinal's robes only on important ceremonial occasions, preferring the plain cassock of a parish priest. Possessions meant nothing to him. All he owned was a record player, some records, and a stack of books. He lived in just two rooms in a city presbytery.

Shortly after arriving in the diocese he was told that one of his students, then in the final year of preparation for the priesthood, had contracted a fatal disease and the seminary authorities acting on medical advice had strongly advised against his ordination. When he asked how long he had to live he was told two years. "I told them," he recalled afterward, "that if he lived just long enough to celebrate one Mass that I'd ordain him."

And that is how Bill Walsh came into my life. When he joined me in St. Joseph's Parish, Wellington, he was aware of the prognosis that he would be dead in two years and from the outset he was a young man in a hurry. His was a highly charged ministry which derived its energy from prayer and especially the praying rather than the studying of Scripture.

Cognoscere oves—getting to know the flock—was a pastoral priority. "It is better to ring door-bells than church-bells," was a favorite dictum of his. Apart from long hours spent with the sick and aged in home and hospital the most striking feature of his ministry was the pastoral care of prisoners. He just about wore a track to Mount Crawford Prison, the largest detention center in the capital city. Here he got to know all the inmates, irrespective of creed or color.

Among the many converts he had under instruction was Martha. She was a young lady who wished keenly to become a Catholic but there was one obstacle—her rooted resistance to all forms of knowledge, religious included. Priest after priest had given her up in despair before Bill took her on. His approach like his preaching was salted with Scripture and relied heavily on storytelling and imagination. So like the Lord he decided to instruct her in parables, and it worked. Of course there were times of extreme frustration, like when he was telling her the story of the Good Samaritan. He went over it with her carefully, as the Lord told it. Then he put it in modern idiom in a contemporary situation.

"Supposing, Martha," he said to her, "you're coming home one evening and you're attacked, robbed, beaten up and left half dead on the pavement, and then the first person who happens to be passing sees you and does nothing. Then a second person comes along. He takes one look at you and crosses to the other side of the street—he doesn't want to know you. Then along comes a Maori. He is full of compassion for you, he hires a taxi and takes you to the hospital. He pays all your expenses and brings you flowers every day. Now Martha," he concluded, "which one of these three was your Good Samaritan?"

She thought for a while, then her face lit up and she said, "The second one!"

Anyway, he persevered and just before he died he baptized Martha and received her into the church. The doctors were right; his priesthood lasted two years almost to the day. I was with him when the end came. Like his life, it too was a living prayer.

The church was full to overflowing for his requiem. They came from every walk of life, amongst them six men in prison garb accompanied by a few officers. Peter McKeefry had considerable difficulty in controlling his emotions during his panegyric, and then as he concluded the prayer of final farewell there was a sudden commotion in the church. Archbishop and congregation looked on in amazement as the prisoners were seen to bolt from their seats. It was not an escape bid; they made straight for the casket which they lifted and carried shoulder high down the church. In the crowd outside I saw a lone figure wiping the tears from her eyes. It was Martha—she had finally recognized the Good Samaritan!

Some years later, as he was seated at his desk talking on the phone to a priest, death came suddenly and unexpectedly to Peter Cardinal McKeefry. While he lived he wrote a last will and testament which was read at his requiem Mass. The will was extremely simple. It consisted of just one sentence:

I declare myself to be possessed of no property
real or personal.

The testament, however, is a self-portrait which has a pertinent message for all of us. It is my final illustration so bear with me as I quote from it.

"The uncertainty of death's hour prompts me to write these few paragraphs, for life has been happy for me, and if death allowed, then I would wish to be able to say to all these words of appreciation. But—and it is a big 'but'—who knows the hour when death comes? So, be it sudden, or long and lingering with diminution of faculties, it would seem better to write now what I would wish to say before death.

"Let me assure everybody that apart from the worries of conscience over my sins, all of my life has been a happy one, and it has been a joy to be amongst priests, religious and laity—to experience the warmth of friendships, to watch their devoted labors and sacrifices, and to know and feel the strength of prayerful support.

"I wish to thank the priests, religious and laity of the Archdiocese of Wellington for all their kindness to me since I came to them. Without their extreme generosity shown so fully, both spiritually and temporally, it would not have been possible to carry the duties of office, and to face the tasks inseparable from it...God be thanked for the privilege to know and work with them.

"Joyfully I greet the diocese of my birth, Christchurch, the diocese of my youth, Dunedin, and the diocese of my priest-hood, Auckland; and to priests, bishops, religious and laity I fully and humbly acknowledge all that they have given me down the years, and the great obligations thereby incurred; and how sadly I admit my failure to have profited by what they gave...

"I beg pardon of all whom I have offended, either through conscious action or through neglect of duty; and in particular I ask forgiveness of those to whom I have been a scandal; and I trust that all in their charity will secure for me, by their prayers, pardon from God for all offenses given by me, or scandal caused through me.

"But let no one think that this is any kind of lament or dirge. It is being written while I feel in the best of health; but I am not blind to the fact that death will come to me as to all others. I have plenty to worry about, but such worries come from my knowing the gravity of my failure before God and man. Apart from that disturbing knowledge, I am content, very happy, and extremely grateful for all the joys that have been mine in my life as priest and Archbishop. My only wish is to let everybody know of my joy, the sincerity of my appreciation of devoted friendships and the warmth of my gratitude.

> Know you the journey that I take?
> Know you the voyage that I make?
> The joy of it one's heart could break.
> No jot of time have I to spare;
> No will to linger anywhere,
> So eager am I to be there,

25. The Singer and the Song

For that the way is hard and long,
For that grey fears upon it throng,
I set my going to a song.
And it is wondrous happy so
Singing, I hurry on—for oh
It is to God—to God I go.

"However, though I have tried to keep a song in my heart all my life, I realize only too keenly that there will be a moment when, instead of a song, my words will be those of Job—'Have pity on me, have pity on me, at least you, my friends, because the hand of the Lord hath touched me.'"

And above the signature, there is the simple wish: "God love, bless and reward everybody."

This valedictory is for all of us, so it will not be resented if I say, by way of postscript, that for us priests our most impressive illustration in the end is ourselves.

Bibliography

Abbott, Walter M., SJ, and Joseph Gallagher, eds. *The Documents of Vatican II*. London—Dublin: Geoffrey Chapman, 1966.

Bausch, William J. *Storytelling—Imagination and Faith*. Mystic, Connecticut: Twenty-Third Publications, 1984.

———. *Take Heart Father*. Mystic, Connecticut: Twenty-Third Publications, 1986.

Good News Bible. Swindon: Bible Societies, 1976.

Brady, Joseph. *In Monavalla*. Dublin: Gill and Macmillan.

Brown, Raymond E., and Ronald Murphy, eds. *Hermeneutics, The Jerome Biblical Commentary*. Englewood Cliffs: Prentice Hall, 1969.

Buber, Martin. *Tales of the Hasidim*. Translated by Olga Marx. Schocken Books Inc., 1957.

Burghardt, Walter J., SJ. *Still Proclaiming Your Wonders*. New York: Paulist Press, 1984.

Castle, Anthony. *Quotes and Anecdotes: An Anthology for Preachers and Teachers*. Kevin Mayhew Ltd., 1979.

———. *More Quotes and Anecdotes: An Anthology for Parish and School*. Fowler Wright (England)/Mercier Press (Ireland), 1986.

Coggan, Donald. *The Sacrament of the Word*. London: Collins Fount Paperbacks, 1987.

De Mellow, Anthony. *Sadhana, a Way to God*. Anand, India: Gujarat Sahitya Prakash, 1978.

Flower, Robin. *The Western Island*. Oxford: Oxford University Press, 1944.

———. *The Irish Tradition*. Oxford: Oxford University Press.

Foley, Gerald. *Empowering the Laity*. New York: Sheed and Ward, 1986.

Gallagher, Michael Paul, SJ. *Free to Believe*. London: Darton, Longman and Todd, 1987.

Gilbert, William S. *Selected Operas*. London: Macmillan, 1949.

Graham, Billy. *Approaching Hoofbeats*. London: Hodder and Stoughton, 1963.

Hume, Basin. *Searching for God*. London: Hodder and Stoughton, 1977.

Hunter, A. M. *The Parables, Then and Now*. London: SCM Press, 1972.

———. *The Parables for Today*. London: SCM Press, 1983.

Joyce, C. A. *A Thought for the Week*. London: Lakeland, 1974.

Link, Mark, SJ. *Illustrated Sunday Homilies*. Valencia, California: Tabor Publishing, 1988.

———. *Illustrated Daily Homilies*. Allen, Texas: Tabor Publishing, 1988.

McCarthy, Flor, SDB. *Sunday and Holyday Liturgies*. Dublin: Dominican Publications, 1984.

———. *Funeral Liturgies*. Dublin: Dominican Publications, 1987.

McKarns, James. *Go Tell Everyone*. New York: Alba House, 1985.

———. *Seldom-Told Bible Tales*. Lima, Ohio: C. S. S. Publishing Co., 1985.

McKenna, Briege, OSC. *Miracles Do Happen*. Dublin: Veritas Publications, 1987.

Muggeridge, Malcolm. *Something Beautiful for God*. London: W. Collins.

O'Connor, Flannery. *Everything That Rises Must Converge*. London: Faber and Faber.

———. *The Violent Bear It Away*. London: Faber and Faber, 1985.

———. *Wise Blood*. London: Faber and Faber, 1980.

———. *An Only Child*. London: Pan Book.

Pearse, Patrick H. *Collected Works of P. H. Pearse*. Dublin: Phoenix, 1917.

Priestland, Gerald. *The Case Against God*. London: Collins, 1984.

Rynne, Stephen. *Father John Hayes*. Dublin: Clonmore and Reynolds, 1960.

Bibliography

Sangster, W. E. *The Craft of Sermon Illustration*. London: Epworth Press, 1954.

————. *Daily Readings from W. E. Sangster*. London: Hodder and Stoughton.

Schillebeeckx, Edward. *Christ, The Sacrament of the Encounter with God*. New York: Sheed and Ward, 1966.

Schweitzer, Albert. *On the Edge of the Primeval Forest*.

Shea, John. *Stories of God*. Chicago: Thomas More Press, 1978.

————. *Stories of Faith*. Chicago: Thomas More Press, 1980.

Spurgeon, Charles H. *Sermons for Special Days and Occasions*. Grand Rapids, Michigan: Baker House, 1984.

Stacy, John. *Preaching Reassessed*. London: Epworth Press, 1977.

Steward, James S. *Preaching*. London: Hodder and Stoughton, 1955.

Stott, John. *Issues Facing Christians Today*. Basingstoke: Marshall, Morgan and Scott, 1984.

————. *The Cross of Christ*. Leicester: Inter Varsity Press, 1986.

Watson, David. *I Believe In The Church*. London: Hodder and Stoughton, 1978.

Waznak, Robert. *Sunday after Sunday—Preaching the Homily as Story*. Ramsey, New Jersey: Paulist Press, 1983.

Wiesel, Elie. *Night*. London: Penguin, 1981.

Index of Scripture References

Index of Themes

Expand Your Storytelling Library

SEASONAL ILLUSTRATIONS FOR PREACHING AND TEACHING

Donald L. Deffner

Paper, $11.95, 176 pages, 5½" x 8½"
ISBN 0-89390-234-9

Preachers and Teachers: Use these illustrations to get your listeners' attention and enrich their understanding of the church year. These short bits will sometimes make listeners laugh and always make them think.

SERMONS FOR SERMON HATERS

Andre Papineau

Paper, $10.95, 144 pages, 5½" x 8½"
ISBN 0-89390-229-2

It's a preacher's dream: to turn on the turned off. That's Andre Papineau's specialty. He's a preacher, a psychotherapist, and an actor. He uses this unique combination of skills to show you how to break open the Gospel in ways that reach even the most jaded.

To receive our current catalog, which lists dozens of story collections and related resources, write to the address shown on the order form below.
